PATTI DICKINSON

# Hollywood the Hard Way

University of Nebraska Press: Lincoln & London

A Cowboy's Journey

Copyright © 1999
by the University
of Nebraska Press
All rights reserved
Manufactured in
the United States
of America ⊗

Library of Congress Cataloging-in-Publication Data
Dickinson, Patti, 1945–
Hollywood the hard way : a cowboy's journey / Patti
Dickinson   p. cm.
ISBN 0-8032-6619-7 (paper : alkaline paper)
1. Cowboys – West (U.S.) – Social life and customs.
2. Van Meter, Jerry – Journeys – West (U.S.)
3. West (U.S.) – Description and travel.   4. Cowboys –
West (U.S.) – Biography.   5. Packhorse camping –
West (U.S.)   6. Guthrie Region (Okla.) – Biography.
I. Title
F596.D53   1999   917.804'33–dc21   99-18423   CIP

This book is dedicated to the dreamer
in all of us, and to
Jerry, whose courage fifty years later
still shines bright.

Courage is not the absence of fear, but the conquest of it.

Anonymous

# CONTENTS

# Acknowledgments

The story of Jerry Van Meter's journey could easily have been lost were it not for the strength of oral history and the cooperation of many helpful people. I would like to thank those individuals whose efforts enabled me to bring the story to light and who assisted with research and verification. To Jerry himself, for his patience with my relentless questioning to get beyond the obvious; to his late wife, Hazel, for her enthusiasm and support; to Elizabeth Eaton Wise and Lindalee Wakely, for their stories and the use of pictures of their famous fathers. Thank you to James, David, William, and Byron Van Meter for their amusing and often poignant insights into the Goodnight and Van Meter families. The thorough genealogical work of the late Lee Goodnight is appreciated as well. I owe a big thank you to Cheryl Rhodes, president of Panhandle Equine Rescue, Inc., my own horse whisperer; to Captain (retired) Kenneth Myatt of the California Highway Patrol for his active participation and research into the history of his organization; and to Lauren Chaiet and Lynne Jackson for their excellent editorial efforts. My heartfelt thanks also go to Julie Woody for sitting down at my table that first day to tell me a story she was sure I should write, and to my husband, David, for his infinite patience and unwavering faith.

# Introduction

I first heard the story of Jerry Van Meter's horseback ride to Hollywood in a friendly little bar on the shores of Flathead Lake in western Montana. Attending a writers' conference nearby, I stopped for lunch along the highway and ordered the Montana-size hamburger the bartender recommended. When the bartender (Julie was her name) discovered my reason for being in the area, she pulled out a chair and sat down at my table – "I've got a story you *have* to write." The details were sketchy, something about a horseback ride a friend of her father's had made to win a bet. I listened, skeptically at first. Although it didn't take her long to relate what she knew, in those few minutes Julie hooked me like a prize catch from the lake's cool waters. I *had* to meet this man and find out the details of his story.

Heroes exist. Disasters highlight their deeds, and we see them briefly on the evening news. But we rarely get to know the ordinary person, the one who lifts him or herself above the crowd by some extraordinary feat. If the man actually did what Julie said, I had a hero in my sights – at least a hero by my definition.

It took me a year to track him down for an interview. He and his wife had left for Arizona for the winter; the following spring he was in a Montana hospital with health problems. It took another six months, but I finally met with Jerry Van Meter in September 1995, almost a year to the day after I first heard his story.

A handsome silver-haired gentleman with a ready smile, Jerry spoke softly with a gentle Oklahoma accent. I told him the story I had heard and asked if it were true. "It is," he said.

He unfolded an old map, touched the stub of a pencil to his tongue, and traced a path across the yellowed paper. Jerry then began to tell me about his journey, his blue eyes mirroring excitement as though it had taken place yesterday instead of over fifty years ago. "It was sure something, all right," he said. By the time he got to the *why* and the famous names responsible for the ride, I silently blessed Julie for interrupting my lunch.

More than a year of research and many lengthy interviews with Jerry and his family have enabled me to recreate the scenes and dialogue that led to his journey and to show what 1945–46 Oklahoma was like and the people involved in this story. Most of the meetings and conversations of that time Jerry vividly remembers. Still, the passage of fifty-plus years cannot help but cause *some* memories to fade, requiring literary license in the few instances of incomplete data or conflicting accounts.

Every attempt has been made to relay the truth, for it is in the truth that the simple beauty of this story lies.

By the early 1890s Oklahoma was divided roughly in half between Oklahoma Territory and Indian Territory. The region was a raw land not yet a part of the Union. Children of that era grew up with stories about Indians, gunfighters, cowboys, cattle drives, and great land runs. By the time Oklahoma became a state in 1907, many of those youngsters were grown, and they passed these same stories on to their own sons and daughters.

As of 1945, farming still involved half of the state's population. Imbued with a rich history of the past, this generation became part of Oklahoma's postwar revival, blending industrialism with a pioneer spirit reflective of the nineteenth century. Like Route 66 – the magical stretch of highway that linked Chicago to Los Angeles – postwar Oklahoma incorporated the best of the old world and the new. People cherished their memories but they embraced the future with open arms.

Oklahomans who came of age in the 1940s revered their grandparents who had come to the territory on horseback or in a prairie schooner but knew their own dreams were tied to the postwar future. They formed a new generation with one foot solidly in each world – a pioneer past, a promising tomorrow.

What follows is the adventure of one such young man. This is the story he told me.

# Mr. Hollywood

*Enid Morning News*, September 17, 1945 // Thousands Line Enid Streets for Colorful Parade // Jimmy Wakely, Monogram Star, Heads Cherokee Strip Entertainment // Goodnight and Eaton End Chisholm Trail Ride to Kick Off 52nd Annual Festival

Jerry Van Meter let Buster have free rein. The quarter horse knew the trails around the ranch as well as his rider did. Jerry never tired of this countryside, the rolling hills, the creeks that snaked their way across the Oklahoma prairie, the wind-blown trees that dotted the horizon. All were as familiar as his own reflection. Family roots, cherished memories, and generations of stories made this landscape home.

Bright after the night's storm, the moonlight danced across the top of fields of golden grass bent by the breeze. Crickets, coyotes, hoot owls, and lowing cattle filled the air with their sounds. Departing clouds scurried southeast toward Arkansas, scattering life-giving rain as they went. Up ahead, porch lights from the Bar R Ranch sent pale slivers of light out across the yard.

The Bar R's five thousand acres sat smack in the middle of the prairie between Enid and Marshall in northwest Oklahoma. Home to Jerry and his grandfather, Rolla Goodnight, the ranch also contained a dozen or so draft and quarter horses, two or three milk cows, numerous cats, dogs, and chickens, eight hundred head of Herefords, and five ranch hands. A good part of the time Rolla's life-long friend, Frank "Pistol Pete" Eaton, lived at the Bar R as well. Everyone said even a blind man could follow the worn trail between Frank's home in nearby Perkins and the Bar R.

As he neared the house Jerry spotted Frank's oversized

cowboy hat and Rolla's six-foot-two-inch frame silhouetted against the house's exterior white siding. The two of them were talking to someone. Buster slowed to a walk and took his own sweet time getting to the gate, finally stopping in front of the house. Jerry recognized the third figure as Jimmy Wakely, another long-time friend of his grandfather's.

Jimmy Wakely, the Hollywood movie cowboy and Monogram Pictures star, and his band had been the main entertainment at the Fifty-Second Annual Cherokee Strip Celebration. The three days of festivities held in Enid in mid-September every year commemorate the 1893 land rush that led pioneers to homestead more than six and a half million acres of former Cherokee tribal hunting grounds in Oklahoma. Clearly the main attraction of the huge event, Wakely had ridden his movie horse, Lucky, at the head of the biggest parade in Enid's history earlier in the day.

Wakely had traded the fancy cowboy clothes he'd worn in the parade for faded jeans and shirt and scuffed boots. He rose as Jerry walked up on the porch. "Nice to see you, Jerry. You've grown up since I last saw you."

Jimmy Wakely and Bing Crosby could have been brothers – similar in height and build, the same handsome face and smooth crooner's voice. At Saturday night's dance Wakely had brought the house down singing "You Can't Break the Chains of Love," his latest Decca release. Afterward he invited everyone, in his easy "I'm just one of you folks" style to see *Saddle Serenade*, his new movie due to come out in two weeks. The appreciative crowd kept him singing on stage for another half hour.

"Your granddad invited me to spend my last night in Oklahoma at a real cattle ranch," Jimmy said, and offered his hand.

"Glad you could make it, Mr. Wakely." Jerry shook his hand. "Sure enjoyed your music at the dance. I didn't think the crowd was ever going to let you quit."

"Call me Jimmy, would you? 'Mister' sounds too formal. Rolla tells me you're the foreman here at the Bar R."

2

"Yes, sir."

Wakely smiled. "Sir. That's right, you've been in the service, haven't you? What branch?"

"The navy," Jerry said softly and looked down at his boots. "Not very long, though. I ah . . . I didn't get to fin . . ." Jerry glanced at his grandfather. "I wasn't in long enough to do any good."

"Well, no need to call me sir, either, Jerry. Just plain old Jimmy will do."

Jerry straightened up and looked at Wakely. "Okay, Jimmy it is. I'd better take care of Buster and get to bed. After camping out for two weeks with these guys on the Chisholm Trail plus three days of celebrating in town, my work is stacked up. Tomorrow's gonna be a big day." Jerry gathered up Buster's reins and started for the barn.

Wakely called after him. "Lucky is in the barn. Would you mind checking on him when you take care of Buster?"

"Be glad to. 'Night everybody."

# 2

## Better See If Hell's Froze Over

*Enid Daily Eagle*, September 17, 1945 // Storm Drops .38" of Rain, Drought Continues // Eisenhower Promises 2.4 Million Troops Home by Christmas // Millions of Vets Expected to Apply for Funds under New GI Bill

Rolla watched as his grandson disappeared into the barn. Neither Jimmy nor Frank had noticed Jerry's embarrassment at the mention of the navy. Yet every time the subject of being in the service came up Jerry reacted the same way. Rolla vividly remembered Jerry's arrival at the Bar R right after his discharge. The shock of seeing him that way still hurt. He came in the dead of winter, thin and drawn and pale as a ghost. Sweat had broken out on his forehead when he struggled up the three steps to the porch and into the house. Trussed in a back brace and in obvious pain, he glanced at his grandfather. "From a baseball game," Jerry half-whispered. He never spoke of it again.

A gust of wind rattled the porch windows. Rolla pushed the painful memory from his mind and breathed deeply the earth's damp fragrance. The autumn evening, interrupted by a fast-moving rainstorm, had given way to air crackling with freshness. Rain clung to the leaves on the big cottonwood near the house, the drops shimmering like twinkling Christmas lights.

Wakely sighed. "Mmmh, you can't buy a perfume as good as the prairie right after a rain." He closed his eyes and smiled. "Plus I can still smell a little bit of fried chicken. You and Frank did a good job on supper. That's the best meal I've had since I left California." A coyote howled in the distance and was soon joined by a chorus. "And I haven't heard coyotes that weren't part of a script in a coon's age. This is heaven, you know that?" Jimmy said, slapping at insects that buzzed around him.

"Won't argue that," Rolla said. "I feel sorry for you, having to go back to California tomorrow."

"Right this minute so do I. It's good to be back home. These folks are sure salt-of-the-earth people."

"They love you, that's for sure," Frank said.

"That's because they think I'm a real cowboy. They're confusing what they see on the screen with guys like you." Wakely drained his glass of iced tea and gestured at the moonlit vista. "What a beautiful sight. Too bad it's disappearing."

Rolla glanced at Jimmy, expecting to see a smile accompany the joke. "What do you mean? What's disappearing?"

"Ranches like this. Dyed-in-the-wool cowboys like you. This whole way of life," Jimmy said.

Surprise also registered on Frank's lined face. "Whoa, partner. You're joshin' us, right?"

"No, Frank, I wish I were," Jimmy said with a shake of his head. "The days of cattle barons are long gone. So are the days of cowhands driving big herds thousands of miles. The only way you're going to see that anymore is if you go to the movies." Wakely poured himself another glass of tea from the pitcher next to his chair. "Like *Cheyenne Roundup* and *The Old Chisholm Trail* I made with Johnny Mack Brown and Tex Ritter, remember?"

"Yeah, but – " Frank's brow furrowed.

"They're all we have left to show what those days were like. I'm sorry to say it, but I believe your way of life at the Bar R is going the same way." Wakely turned to Rolla. "Can you name me one cattleman today in Oklahoma or Texas who's anything like your cousin, Charlie Goodnight?"

Rolla thought for a moment. "Well . . . not right off hand," he said, rubbing his chin. "I'll admit men were a might different in the old days. Charlie was a renegade, reckless as all get out, but smarter 'n a whip. He was to cattle in the 1800s what Frank Phillips was to oil in the 1900s." Rolla pictured Charlie and chuckled. "He sure loved to joke. One time somebody took his photograph standing by a buffalo, their heads right together. When he saw the picture he cussed up a blue streak, the gist of which was that the damn thing was near as good looking as him. Charlie taught me everything I know about the cattle business," Rolla said. "I never would have made it through the Depression and hung onto the Bar R if it wasn't for him. I used everything he taught me."

Jerry called out from the dimly lit bunkhouse across the yard, "Lucky seems right at home, Jimmy. See y'all in the morning."

Rolla acknowledged his grandson's call with a wave. He turned to Wakely. "When I was fourteen I left my folks in Kansas and rode to the Palo Duro, Charlie's ranch in the Texas Panhandle. I wanted to be a cowboy just like him. And he taught me good. Being a rancher and a cowboy is all I know. If what you're saying is true, what's that say about my life? Frank's, too."

"It says you and Frank are a special breed of men – which you damn sure are – and you've lived a period of history that won't ever be again." Wakely pointed to the landscape. "This country is changing fast now that the war is over. My band and I travel all over, so I see it. Big change. Soldiers already home are getting married and moving to cities so they can go to college under the new GI Bill. Building is booming. Families are selling their farms right and left, moving to the city. And this is just the beginning."

"The beginning of what?" Frank asked.

"The future, Frank. Seems like the United States is beginning to wake up from a long sleep – first the Depression, then four years of sacrifice waiting until we finished with the war. Now that it's over people don't want things to go back to the way they were. They want a better life. I'm telling you, when

6

the rest of the troops get home they're going to do the same thing – kiss farm life goodbye and move to Oklahoma City, Tulsa, or Muskogee. They're going to get factory jobs, maybe build a house and buy a new car. It's already happening in California. People are flocking into L.A. – all of southern California – like moths to a flame. Cities everywhere are exploding overnight." Wakely's expression, at first grim, turned to a smile. "I hate to be the one to break the news to you, but before long it's going to happen here, too. Then you'll have to go to the theater in Enid and pay money to see me or Gene Autry or Roy Rogers doing the stuff you've been doing all your lives."

Frank gazed at Wakely, his amusement barely concealed. "Funny, you got a smile on your face but you don't sound like you're joshin'."

An Australian shepherd appeared out of the darkness, ambled up onto the porch then went to each man looking to be petted. The dog settled down at Rolla's feet. "I got a crew of five good young cowboys," Rolla said. "I don't see them hoppin' up and down to leave."

Wakely reached over and scratched the dog's neck. "You know as well as I do they're not near the caliber of cowboy you and Frank are."

Rolla wanted very much to dismiss what Jimmy said, but he knew better. At least once a month the Enid or Guthrie papers carried a story about Jimmy Wakely and his band playing in some city around the country. *He's in a better position than me to see change taking place. And Jimmy's not one to say something important like that if he didn't believe it.* Rolla suddenly wished their conversation hadn't taken this turn; it gave him an uneasy feeling.

Jimmy insisted. "Be honest now. Are you telling me your cowboys would know how to pull a cow out of quicksand or stop a stampede in the middle of a norther'? Could they stand eating beans and bacon three meals a day for three months? You know very well they couldn't. And not a one of them could sit in the saddle for fifteen hundred miles like you guys did."

"You paint a sorry picture, Jimmy, but when you talk cowboy you're talking Charlie Goodnight. One of a kind, that man," Frank said, his handlebar mustache shifting angles as he spoke. "Always thunderin' around on them bow legs, cussin' up a storm. He could cuss better 'n any man I ever knew. 'Course when you own a million acres and run a hundred thousand head of cattle on your ranch you can purty much talk like you want."

"I didn't know you knew him, Frank," Jimmy said.

"I surely did. My uncle, Nick Eaton, had a spread on Running Water Creek in Texas. He and Charlie was friends. Remember, Rolla, that time we rode with Nick and Charlie and Deaf Smith to Caldwell, Kansas? Charlie rode right along, wrangling like one of us. He was a tough old bugger. I run across lots of men in my time – lawmen, good Indians, bad Indians, and a whole passel of gunfighters 'n thieves. Colt Younger and his bunch and Belle Starr, I knew all of them. Every one of 'em robbed for a livin', even Belle."

Jimmy slapped his thigh. "I'll be damned. You knew *them*?"

"Sure 'nuf. You couldn't call one of them people a legend except maybe Pat Garrett. He was the finest lawman I ever run into. Killed Billy the Kid, you know. But Charlie Goodnight, now we're talkin' legend. Yessiree. The things I learned from him saved my hide more than once."

Lightning flashed off in the distance, its retreating light briefly illuminating the contour of the prairie. Frank went into the house and returned with three mugs of coffee. He handed one to Rolla and another to Wakely.

"Thanks," Jimmy said. "*You* lived with him, Rolla, what was Charlie like? I've read about some of the things he did, but what kind of man was he?"

Rolla sipped his coffee thoughtfully. "Fearless. Charlie wasn't afraid of nothing or nobody. He was a Texas Ranger when he was young. And Charlie never got tired like an ordinary man. Even as a kid I had a hard time keeping up with

8

him. He was a cattleman through and through. That's all he thought about. He ate, drank, and slept cattle. When we weren't riding he read about cattle or talked to me about the cattle business, always trying to improve the herd. And Charlie was as practical as they come. You know those chuck wagons you use in the movies?"

Wakely nodded. "Sure. They come with a cantankerous cook like Gabby Hayes who dishes out make-believe grub and medicine and gives advice whether you want it or not."

"Well, ever-practical Charlie Goodnight invented the chuck wagon. He took a military supply wagon and changed it around, then equipped it for cookin' so they could use it on long cattle drives."

"Well I never knew that," Jimmy said.

"I ain't sure we'll ever see a man like him again," Frank said and then downed the last of his coffee.

Rolla raised his mug in a toast. "Charlie Goodnight was bigger than life: tough, bull-headed, always ready for adventure. He loved ranchin' more 'n anything. I'm proud to say I'm part of that tradition. It's something I'd like to pass on to my grandson. I'm not crazy about hearing the way of life I've spent seventy-five years livin' is damned near gone."

"I said I didn't like being the one to tell you," Jimmy shrugged.

"Wait a minute. Are you saying cowboyin' is dead all together?" Frank asked. The dog raised his head at Frank's sharp voice.

"Not just cowboyin', Frank," Jimmy said. He gestured at the Bar R. "Family ranching, this whole way of life. There just aren't any men around like you guys anymore . . ."

Frank stood up and pointed his gnarled finger at Wakely. "Nosiree bob. People are always gonna eat steak. And if you're runnin' cattle you need horses. Horses have to have cowboys ridin' 'em. That ain't gonna change and that's all I got to say." Muttering something about needing more coffee, Frank disappeared into the house with a slap of the screen door.

Rolla decided he'd heard enough. "Now you listen, Mr. Hollywood. I got somebody working for me that's as good a cowboy as me 'n Frank ever was – my grandson, Jerry. He can ride from here to hell and gone, break a horse, ride a bull, and rope a cow with the best of 'em."

Frank returned with the coffee pot and started to fill Rolla's mug. "Hold that danged thing still or I'm gonna pour this down your boot," he said. Frank refilled their mugs and set down the pot. "I heard what Rolla said about Jerry and he's right. Old-time cowboys like us got nothin' on that boy."

Wakely laughed. "Glory be. Rolla Goodnight and Frank Eaton agreeing on something? You're only saying that because he's your grandson, Rolla. Jerry's awfully young. I don't see how he could be *that* good."

Rolla stood up to his full height, punctuating the air with his forefinger as he spoke. "I am not saying it because he's my grandson, I am saying it because it is the truth," he said hotly. "You don't know what that boy's been through. He's tough as they come. And not only that, he's got Goodnight blood runnin' in his veins. He learned cowboyin' from Frank 'n me from the time he could walk. Why, he took to it like a duck to water. Jerry is a cowboy clean through." Rolla leaned over, locking eyes with Jimmy, his voice measured. "I am willing to put my money where my mouth is. Are you?"

"Hot damn, I'm likin' this now," Frank said, slapping his thigh.

Wakely whistled. "I can't believe it, a Goodnight making a bet? I'd better check to see if hell's froze over." Jimmy was still chuckling as he and Rolla shook hands. "What kinda money are we talking about, Rolla?"

10

# 3

## The Bet

*Enid Morning News*, September 18, 1945 // Oklahoma Flour Mills Face Shutdown – Wheat Shortage // Swift Reconversion Reduces Government Orders to Factories by 80% // New DDT Insect Spray Hits Market, Dubbed "New Wonder of the Earth"

Smoke poured out of the stovepipe in the ranch house roof. A wonderful aroma wafted out through the screen door as Jerry approached the house for dinner. He loved this time of year. One of the best months in Oklahoma, September meant warm days and nights and often an unexpected storm that freshened and cooled the air – like the one last night. For Jerry, the small white frame house and its inviting porch conjured up lively memories of a time when his grandmother, Ida, was alive. He and his four brothers would play in the giant barn and later gather around the kitchen table for one of Grandma Ida's great meals. She had cooked on the same Majestic wood stove that Rolla still used.

Jerry arrived at six p.m. sharp; Rolla Goodnight admired promptness as much as he did cleanliness. Frank was setting the table when Jerry walked in; he looked up and smiled. Dressed in clean, pressed clothes, Frank wore his shiny gray hair in his customary two long braids.

Rolla and Frank good-naturedly wrangled over the way to do everything, from shoeing a horse to making a pot of beans, but in their sixty-three years of friendship they both had become good cooks. Jerry knew what they had prepared even before he saw the pot roast; its aroma made his mouth water. A pitcher of iced tea sat next to several bowls of food on the table, its rivulets of condensation cascading down the pitcher's side and depositing a ring of moisture on the blue tablecloth.

The three men spent the next few minutes swapping bowls and carrying on idle conversation. Finally they began to eat. Jerry was quietly enjoying his supper when he began to feel something strange. He looked up. Both men were staring at him. "What's going on? Did I miss something?"

Frank chuckled. "You shoulda stuck around last night."

"I made a bet with Jimmy Wakely," Rolla said. The characteristic twinkle in his eyes was gone, replaced by a serious expression. Jerry shot Frank a questioning glance and then smiled, relieved to see Frank's familiar grin. It lit up his weathered face, already made impish by his crossed left eye.

Rolla spoke up. "You know, Jerry, I don't believe in gambling. I've never done anything like this in my life. But Jimmy spouted all this stuff about cities exploding and ranching going to hell. He sounded so sure about it. Besides, it's the principle. Anyway, one thing led to another and I bet him."

"Bet him what?" Jerry said calmly and resumed eating.

"Now when I tell you, don't go gettin' in a lather. It won't be until spring. I bet Jimmy you would make a little ride. He bet you couldn't do it."

"How *little* of a ride?"

Frank, silently watching the exchange, piped up. "Movie star country, boy. Hollywood, California."

Jerry's fork paused in midair. "Hollywood? We're halfway across the country from Hollywood."

Rolla nodded. "Jimmy said cowboyin' is dead. He says our whole way of life is all but gone. Worse yet, he says there's not a cowboy around anymore worth his salt. That didn't sit right with me."

"I still don't see what Hollywood has to do with it."

Rolla ran his finger along an imaginary line on the tablecloth. "Well, it's about fifteen hundred miles to Hollywood, and Jimmy lives not far from there. Frank 'n me figured the

12

stretch of Goodnight-Loving Trail between the Brazos and Denver was about that long. It used to take us three months to take a herd that far, depending on weather and how much trouble we run into. Jimmy and I hassled back and forth and I finally said that without a bunch of cows to slow you down you could ride to Hollywood in fifty days, maybe less."

"Yessiree, that's what he said. I heard it with my own ears." Frank was eating fast, talking between bites.

Jerry sat quietly, letting the words sink in. *Grandpa made a bet based on me being tough. I'm not tough. If I were I'd be a navy pilot by now. I have no idea if I can do that.* Jerry cleared his throat. "Fifteen hundred miles in fifty days? That's thirty miles a day, every day for almost two months." *That doesn't leave any room if something goes wrong. If I got hurt I could mess up my back for good. The navy all over again.*

His grandfather and Frank were talking but Jerry didn't hear them. The slow fire started in his gut again when he thought about the random, rotten luck. Anger quickly surfaced, then a darker feeling, one even more disturbing, stirred within him; it was a feeling Jerry thought he'd laid to rest. At the mention of a challenge, any challenge that put him to the test, fear galloped back into Jerry's mind like a wild mustang. *I don't want any more life-altering surprises, no more hospitals and pain, no more being afraid I'll never walk again.*

Apprentice Seaman Jerry Van Meter had reported to the U.S. Navy Air Corps at Warrensburg State Teachers College in Missouri one week after he graduated from Guthrie High School in Guthrie, Oklahoma. He and his squadron reported for duty, anxious to learn about weather, navigation, and elementary aviation – a tough program. Jerry studied hard. Upon completion he would graduate to flight school in Pensacola and learn to fly P-40s or Curtis Interceptors for the navy. That's what he'd hoped for and dreamed about until the day of the intersquadron baseball game.

When the smelling salts brought him around, the doctor

asked Jerry if he could wiggle his toes. Jerry tried but nothing happened. The ensign who doubled as Jerry's weather instructor and part-time coach, and big Moose Malone, the center fielder who had run into him, stood next to the doctor at the end of the bed. All three faces were white as sheets. "Try one more time, Jerry," the doctor said. Jerry tried again. Pain swamped his entire body, radiating from the base of his skull down through his back and into every limb. Sweat broke out on his forehead as he kept trying. Then his toes moved slightly. When they did, he saw relief flood each of their faces.

Jerry's dream of being a navy fighter pilot and after the war flying for one of the airlines had all vanished in the time it had taken to catch a baseball. He didn't remember the collision, or being carried off on a stretcher, or the ambulance ride to the Warrensburg hospital. He did remember waking up in a fog, his body aching all over, and a terrible, terrible headache. Three frightening months of pain followed, three months of wondering if he would be able to walk again. His squadron buddies dropped by for an occasional visit but never stayed long. Why would they? Jerry lay flat on his back, head and neck immobilized by heavy traction. Then "the Meeting."

If he closed his eyes Jerry could still picture the grave expression on his squadron commander's face.

"The doctor wants to transfer you to the Great Lakes Naval Hospital in Chicago, Jerry. They have better facilities to deal with this sort of problem. Maybe they can help you without surgery. The three discs you ruptured are going to take special treatment. I'm sorry, son. You'll lose too much time as a result of this injury. There's no way you can catch up with the program. The navy will give you an honorable discharge, but your navy career is over."

*Your navy career is over* – those five words dashed a dream. Despair grabbed the pit of his stomach. *My future shot to hell.* Jerry took a deep breath and cleared his throat, suddenly aware that Rolla and Frank were staring at him with identical puzzled expressions. "I'll have to think about this, Grandpa," Jerry said hoarsely.

"But Jerry, I already made the bet. I told Jimmy you'd do it." Jerry could hear the disappointment and frustration in his grandfather's voice and see it on his face.

Jerry jumped to his feet. "I'm sorry." He grabbed his hat from the back of the chair and bolted for the door.

As the screen door snapped shut, Jerry heard his grandfather's words: "What in the world is the matter with that boy?"

Jerry saddled Buster and rode out on the prairie, heading where he always went when he wanted to be alone. Buster's steady canter took them to a thin, gouged out streambed lined with red cedars, cottonwoods, and elms. They arrived just as the sun began its final descent toward the horizon.

Trail Creek served as Jerry's place of solace. Nestled at the convergence of two low hills, it looked out over the prairie. Lush and green in the spring, the hills were gold now, washed with the colors of the setting sun. The ever-present wind rustled the leaves of the trees, scattering them along the dry creekbed. Jerry sat down with his back against a bent cedar, watching as Buster began to graze. The sun's red and orange fingers reached out from the horizon, daring him to look west, taunting him for being afraid. Jerry squinted as the colors deepened. "Damn, I hate this feeling," he said to the horse. "*Boy*. Grandpa and Frank always call me *boy*. If I don't make the ride I'll never be more than that in their minds."

Buster moved close and nudged his shoulder. "You ever been afraid, Buster? I don't think Grandpa and Frank have. How could I admit being scared to the likes of them? They have no idea how lucky I am just to be walking. After all the things they've done in their lives there's no way they could understand. If I try this and fail I'm not worth my salt. If I don't try I'm a coward." Buster moved away; Jerry could tell he wanted to go back to the ranch. It was dark by the time Jerry rode back to the Bar R. He wanted to forget the navy and the year of pain, forget wondering whether he'd ever feel good again. He wanted to be courageous and see that his grandfather and Frank were proud of him. Instead he'd told them he had to think about it, and there was no mistaking the look on their faces.

# 4

## The Truth Comes Out

*Enid Daily Eagle*, September 19, 1945 // 900,000 Shares Traded in Stock Market Dip // Oklahoma Cowboy Champion to Be Named in 3-Day Event // Sammy Snead in Lead for $10,000 Prize, Southwest Invitation Golf Tourney

Not one to avoid confrontations, Jerry approached his grandfather first thing Wednesday morning. He found Rolla and Frank in the barn working on the Farm-All tractor, arguing about the best way to fix it. Frank had his six guns already strapped on and he seemed to be winning. "Now listen here, I'm older 'n you, and I was fixin' these things when you was still in didies."

Rolla looked down at Frank, who was a good six inches shorter than he. "You're only ten dadgum years older and I can fix this tractor in my sleep, why I – "

"Good morning, Grandpa. You too, Frank."

An instant smile appeared on Frank's face. "Top of the mornin', boy. You feelin' better?"

"Don't ask how he's feelin' right off. Don't you know nothing?" Rolla looked at Jerry, his expression guarded. "Mornin', boy."

Rolla and Frank stood looking at Jerry expectantly. Like mismatched bookends – one short, one tall – they had been riding, ranching, and cowboying together since 1885. Cowboys through and through, Rolla and Frank believed in Jerry, landing him at this critical point where he needed to make a decision. Jerry remembered running to keep up with the two of them from the time he could walk. Forever imprinted in his mind as a pair, here they stood side by side like two halves of a

17

circle that didn't match, imperfect but inseparable. And he loved them both.

"It's both of you calling me *boy* that I'd like to talk about, plus I want to tell you something." Jerry sat down on a bale of hay and motioned for them to do the same. Both men sat down across from him, glancing furtively at each other and then down at their boots like elderly Huck Finns dreading a lecture. "I've never told you about the navy, about what happened. I'd like for you to hear it."

Frank leaned forward, his elbows resting on his knees, listening, nodding that he understood, looking sad when Jerry told him what his commander had said. Rolla leaned back against a post, his chin cupped in his hand as he weighed each word. Jerry told them about going up to catch the ball and colliding with Moose Malone, then waking up in pain and the doctors not being sure he'd walk again. He spoke about his hopes for a flying career, about his anger and bitter disappointment when his dream vanished in the blink of an eye. For the first time since it happened Jerry poured out the doubt and anguish the accident had caused, and how the prospect of this ride brought it all back. "My buddies are finishing up flight school in Pensacola right about now, wearing wings on their chests. I should be there with them."

"Well, I'll be," Frank said. "I never give it a thought how that changed things for you."

"I always wondered what really happened. I'm glad you finally said something," Rolla said. He started to rise.

Jerry held up his hand, a signal to wait. "I don't know how else to tell you this except to just say it. You two calling me *boy* doesn't help."

Their identical expressions towards each other with open mouths and raised eyebrows made Jerry smile. Frank spoke up first. "Do I call you that?"

Jerry nodded.

"Well I'll be dawg, must be habit. It don't mean I think of you that way. Why, you shoulda heard your grandpa 'n me tellin' Jimmy what a fine cowboy you are. We both said us old cowboys got nothin' on you, didn't we Rolla?"

Rolla seemed not to hear him; he squinted at Jerry. "Is that why you had to think about going on the ride? Because you got hurt and didn't get to fly? You think Frank 'n me consider you a boy because of that?"

Jerry looked down. "I said I had to think about it because I'm not sure I can make it without messing up my back. I don't know why you call me boy."

Rolla's voice softened. "Maybe the good Lord never meant for you to fly, Jerry. Sometimes bad things happen, but it's like riding a bronc. You can't let it make you afraid. You are the best cowboy in these parts. Frank 'n me know it. The ranch hands know it. Everybody knows it. That's something to be proud of. You 'n me are Goodnights. We don't let anything stop us. Why, I never had a body work harder for me – hurt back and all – than you." Ordinarily Rolla was a man of few words except when he and Frank recounted one of their escapades or he got going on politics. Rolla got up from the bale of hay and paced back and forth between Jerry and Frank. "If you don't like us callin' you boy, speak your mind. Say dammitall, don't call me that." Rolla looked at Frank questioningly; Frank nodded. Rolla stopped walking and turned his intense blue eyes on Jerry. "You can do this ride, Jerry. Now that I know the whole story about the navy I think you need to do it, to prove to yourself what Frank 'n me already know – that you can."

Jerry could feel his grandfather's excitement building. "Jimmy said this country is changing fast. If he's right this may be your only chance to do something like this. Far as I know nobody's ever done it before. You remember me telling you how Charlie Goodnight loved adventures? Well, Frank and me had lots of 'em in our day. We look back on those as some of the best times we ever had."

"You always liked hearin' about 'em," Frank said. Jerry nodded.

"Well that's what this is, the chance of a lifetime. Your own adventure."

"But, what if – "

Rolla shook his head. "If something happens along the way you'll handle it. It'll come natural what to do, and you'll do it. You can show Jimmy Wakely and the rest of them Hollywood cowboys what being a Goodnight means, what being a *real* cowboy is."

Jerry stood up and put his hands on his hips. He and Rolla eyed each other. Frank rose, looking first at one and then the other as though he were watching a tennis match. "Well?" Rolla said.

Jerry glanced at Frank then back at his grandfather. "Dammitall, I don't want either one of you calling me boy anymore."

Rolla nodded emphatically. "You won't hear that from me again."

"Me neither," Frank echoed.

"Thank you," Jerry said quietly.

Rolla and Frank smiled, different faces but each with the same message in their eyes. Two cantankerous, charismatic, funny, hardworking men to whom the word "cowboy" meant honor and courage. Men of integrity spawned in a wild, lawless era that slid into history on industrial-greased skids. Jerry realized the two of them could adapt only so far. Rolla, who was seventy-five, and Frank, at eighty-five, didn't want to hear that everything they had once been and stood for would soon be forgotten, remembered only in movies. They don't deserve that, Jerry thought. He sensed it was up to him to capture time and hold onto it for them. *I must be loco. Anything can happen. I'm probably making the biggest mistake of my life.*

Jerry glanced over at Buster, still in his stall. "That horse wouldn't make it to the Texas border, let alone all the way to Hollywood."

Rolla and Frank stared at him with non-comprehending looks. Then Frank broke into a grin, stepped forward and slapped Jerry on the shoulder. "I'm proud of you, b – , Jerry, real proud."

Rolla smiled and offered his hand. "Me, too, son. Is it okay if I still call you that once in a while?"

Jerry shook his outstretched hand. "That's fine, Grandpa."

Frank cleared his throat. "I hate to break up this lovin' moment, but I got somethin' important to say." He had a dead-serious look on his face. "I got a horse that can make it to Hollywood and then some, that mare of mine, Fancy."

"I couldn't borrow your horse, Frank," Jerry said. "What would you ride?"

"I'll ride that buckskin we broke this spring. Besides, I'm not talkin' about you borrowin' anything. She's yours." Frank's eyes sparkled with excitement.

"Fancy is a beautiful horse. That's way too much."

"She's an Osage Indian pony, Jerry. Once I give her to you I can't take her back. I'd run into terrible luck." Frank shook his head vigorously, his braids flopping back and forth. "No more talk about this, hear?"

"Well, then, thanks to Frank here I've got the horse," Jerry said. "So, how much money do I have to worry about you losing?" He looked at his grandfather.

Rolla slapped Frank on the back, a smile lighting up his face. "You ornery old cuss. For once you're right. Fancy's perfect for the ride." Rolla turned to Jerry. "Don't concern yourself about the money. That's between me and Mr. Hollywood. I ain't worried. The bet's important, but this is about somethin' a whole lot bigger 'n money. Jimmy thinks movie cowboys are all that's left. Hogwash! I say cowboyin' is still a good way of life, somethin' to be proud of. *That's* what this is about."

Jerry shook his head at the decision he'd just made. "Riding a horse to Hollywood, even one as good as Fancy, is damned sure getting there the hard way. But the two of you are right.

I've been training for this my whole life without even realizing it. You and Frank taught me everything I need to get me there."

The three headed for the ranch house for breakfast, with Jerry walking in the middle. He could feel Frank's excitement. Frank stepped even livelier than usual and he couldn't stop talking.

"Now, we got the winter to brush up on his cowboyin'," Frank said as they neared the house. "Think that's enough time, Rolla?"

"It will be if you let *me* do it," Rolla said in a droll voice. "Listen here, I was cowboyin' when you was in didies. There ain't no way I'm gonna let *you* be in charge."

*My God, what have I gotten myself into?*

# 5

## Travel Light, It's a Race against Time

*United Press Service*, December 1945 // Synthetic Oil Developed, Two-City Tryout in East Planned // Automotive Engineers Predict 1947 Production of Rear Engine Passenger Car // Plastic Foam, Secret War Material, Hits Commercial Market

Jerry's ride, his route, and what he should take dominated Rolla and Frank's conversations during the entire winter, conversations that turned lively at times and were usually followed by laughter. Frank rarely rode back to his Perkins home, fearful that Rolla would "mess up Jerry's training." Their planning sessions invariably turned into "do you remember that time we . . ." so Jerry let them talk. He pored over maps, mentally trying to anticipate problems, making notes about the terrain, and logging distances between campsites and supply stops.

The Oklahoma prairie contained many large ranches, but for the most part the state remained open rangeland dissected by country dirt roads. Jerry assumed the Texas panhandle would be the same. He planned to ride southwest across open country until he intersected Route 66, then follow 66 all the way to Amarillo where he could stock up on supplies. After visiting Charlie Goodnight's former ranch in the Palo Duro Canyon he would drop farther south and travel over the Llano Estacado – the high plains of New Mexico – to the base of the Rockies. Riding cross-country, Jerry planned to hunt and fish along the way. He charted his route to pass through a town at least every four days when his supplies would need replenishing. *Travel light, it's a race against time.*

Jerry's "training" with Rolla and Frank proved to be good medicine for helping him forget flying, forget his back injury and the navy. Frank practiced the fast-draw with him several hours every day with empty Colt .45s until Jerry could draw lightning fast. And each day when they finished, his grandfather tossed tin cans into the air and had Jerry fire at them with his Winchester until he did not miss. "Sometimes you only get one shot at a rabbit or a quail. I don't want you to go hungry," Rolla said.

Working with five-year-old Fancy proved to be even better medicine for him. A pinto, Fancy stood sixteen hands high with sturdy white legs and a white blaze. She had a slick coat, broad, red-brown breast and neck, pure white flanks, and wide, brown hindquarters. Fancy followed Jerry around like an eleven-hundred-pound puppy and learned to respond to his voice commands quicker than any horse he'd ever trained. Fancy also craved attention. She nudged Jerry if he ignored her. With her wide-set eyes, brown forelock, and white and brown mane that followed exactly the break in her coloring, Fancy was indeed a beautiful horse – and tireless. She astounded Jerry with her stamina and speed. But the name Fancy didn't fit; it sounded too prissy. She loved water; she liked to roll in dirt or mud; it didn't matter. Ornery when she wanted to be, playful, always hungry, she was anything but fancy. Jerry had timed her. She could "fan right on down the road" – that is, she had a running walk of eight miles an hour, faster than any horse he'd ever seen. He asked Frank if he could shorten her name to Fan.

"She belongs to you now. You can call her Matilda if you want," Frank said. "She'll get you there, but I'm tellin' you that horse'll eat a swath of grass from here to California wide enough to see from one of them aeroplanes."

Jerry laughed and patted the mare's flank. "Okay, Fan. Eat your way to California, but we just have to make sure we get there in fifty days – together."

24

Jerry took a week off at Christmas and went home to Guthrie, his first holiday with his parents since he'd left for Missouri. Both parents worked at Tinker Air Field in Oklahoma City, but Edna Van Meter always made Christmas special. She and Vearl and the boys had decorated a tree. Everyone had gifts, and she cooked a huge dinner of turkey, dressing and gravy, and three kinds of pie, filling the house with delicious smells. "Grandpa and Frank are good cooks, so don't tell them I said this, but this is the best meal I've had in a year," Jerry told her.

The whole family was there except for his eldest brother, Jimmy, who was still in the navy flying transports between California and Guam. The other boys clamored for Jerry's attention. Bill, who was twelve, showed him newspaper clippings about his hero, Bob Feller, just returning from a four-year hitch in the navy to pitch again for the Cleveland Indians. Sixteen-year-old David laid out possum and skunk hides he'd prepared for sale and then he and Jerry pored over the latest comic books that David had gotten from the Guthrie Owl Drug. Byron, eleven, made Jerry practice fast-draws with him and then begged to go on the ride to California. Jerry's father refused to discuss the trip.

Vearl Van Meter was handsome and athletic, but a serious man. A talented baseball player who had made it as far as the minor leagues, he never got any farther. An impending war, a wife, five sons, and an eighty-acre farm precluded a career in professional baseball. The boys helped him tend the family's four milk cows, work the horses and mules, and care for the huge flock of chickens that provided a steady income from local stores. Vearl taught them to hunt and fish, to play baseball, and other practical things boys should know, like how to fix things around the farm. But what he wanted most was for his sons to go to college and excel in sports. Ill with ulcers, Vearl spent most of his spare time reading. Though he never shared in Jerry's and Byron's love of horses, Edna Goodnight Van Meter did; she was an accomplished rider.

25

Edna had inherited her father Rolla's happy nature as well as his blond, blue-eyed good looks. Slender and strong, Edna could ride, can vegetables and fruits, cook, and outrun all her kids at tag or hide and seek. She admired Norman Rockwell's art and loved nothing better than gathering Vearl and the boys around the kitchen table at night for pie while they listened to "Fibber McGee and Molly" or "Gene Autry's Melody Ranch" on the radio.

In a rare moment alone at that table before returning to the Bar R, Jerry talked to his mother about the ride. She sat peeling apples into a bowl, sometimes glancing at her son. "You seem uncertain, Jerry. So why are you doing it?"

"You know how Grandpa and Frank are. This is really important to them. They're as excited as a couple of kids. You think I'm making a mistake?"

"I know your grandfather and Frank only too well. What I think is, don't do it unless it's *your* dream. Not for anyone but yourself."

"How about it, Mom, you think I can make it?"

Edna smiled. "You've wanted to be a cowboy, like Dad and Frank, since you could walk. One minute you were riding a stick horse, and the next thing I knew they had you handling a real one fifteen hands high, and you six years old." His mother got up and washed her hands and came back with two coffees. "After they'd taught you to ride and rope, hunt and track – all the things they loved – you upped and decided you wanted to be a pilot. You and Jimmy. Then the two of you built those models and flew them, talking nothing but airplanes, airplanes, airplanes. Dad and Frank were crushed. They'll get over it. If you're only doing it for them, don't."

"You didn't answer my question. Do you believe I can make it?"

Edna covered his hand with her own. "Remember when you wanted to be Buck Rogers and fly to the moon? I might have to think on that. Not this. I know you can make it, son, but you're the one who has to believe it, not me."

Jerry rode Fan the fifty miles back to the Bar R in a norther'. Blown by a wind straight out of the north, the freezing rain came at them horizontally in sheets. Jerry lowered his hat and pulled his rain slicker tighter. "A little test," he said to Fan. She acted like she was out for a Sunday romp, oblivious to the conditions.

They got back to the Bar R at dusk. Jerry dried her off and brushed her. "This was only one day, not fifty. But as bad as it was we made it in seven hours, easy." He put Fan's blanket on and gave her some rolled oats and hay. "You're making this trip seem a lot more possible, girl."

During the next months Jerry used the ranch quarter horses for his work, but as soon as he finished each day he trained with Fan. Finding rock-strewn trails on the Bar R's varied terrain they rode up and down hills and through its canyons. Fan pranced, she rolled in the mud, and she ate.

They went out in storms, into swollen rivers, and rode at all hours of the day and night. Fan wasn't afraid of deep water or fast currents. And each day when he took care of her Jerry poured out his hopes and misgivings, his restless feelings. Fan yawned; she slept; she looked at Jerry with attentive eyes, swishing her tail, flicking her ears back and forth. He accepted her behavior as nonverbal assent.

Jerry celebrated his twentieth birthday on February 13, 1946. He now wore the special belt on his back only when he did heavy work. Unaware of the subtle shift taking place in his feelings about the ride, visions of adventure replaced fear. He imagined living on the trail like Frank and Rolla had, like Jesse Chisholm and Charlie Goodnight and all the cowboys before them. In his daydreams Jerry conquered every obstacle; he envisioned riding triumphantly into warm, sunny Hollywood with palm-lined boulevards to mark his way.

They trained until Jerry completed his spring work. At that point it seemed pointless to train any more. The horse never faltered; she performed like a champion. The last day of

27

April 1946 Fan had drunk her fill of water and stood swishing her tail, patiently waiting while he finished brushing her. She looked at Jerry, her expression and demeanor indicating she wanted her hay and oats.

"So, you want dinner, do you? Have I trained you or is it the other way around?" He stroked her withers as she devoured her hay. "Dammitall, Fan, we can do this ride."

The pinto stared at him as she chomped through her hay.

"It started out as Grandpa's dream, but I can feel it. You were born to make this ride, Fan. So was I."

# 6

# Final Preparations

*The Clinton Daily News,* May 2, 1946 // Standard Oil Survey Declares Jet Planes Impractical for Peacetime Aviation // Missouri Sheriff Sues Oklahoma Sheriff over 600 Fifths of Confiscated Liquor

Jerry spent his last day at the Bar R, Thursday, May 2, 1946, getting his supplies ready for the trip. He gathered up a bedroll, rain slicker, a one-gallon canteen of water, maps, compass, a pair of Finch pliers, a frying pan, coffee pot, and enough food staples for a few days, including a pint jar of sourdough biscuit starter. Finally he loaded twenty pounds of grain, a box of salt, two extra horseshoes, and a blanket for Fan.

The ranch hands slapped Jerry on the back and laughingly warned him, "Be careful of them Hollywood starlets. If you see Lana Turner or Rita Hayworth, get us a pinup picture, will ya?" Jerry promised he would.

His grandfather motioned Jerry to follow him into the house. Rolla went into his bedroom and returned with an unwrapped box. "You'll be needing these," he said.

"I can't believe this, Grandpa." Jerry lifted a pair of hand-tooled silver spurs, one of his grandfather's prized possessions, out of the box. "These are the spurs Elmer Spark made especially for you." The box also held one hundred fifty dollars, the equivalent of a month's pay, and twenty silver dollars.

Rolla nodded. "I want you to have the spurs. Call your Mama once in a while, let us know you're all right, hear?" Jerry stood staring at the spurs. He heard the screen door bang shut; his grandfather had exited. Taking a last look around the kitchen Jerry tried to stamp its familiar sights and smells into his memory – at the moment, coffee and bacon with a little floor wax thrown in. The old linoleum glistened in the morning sun. Jerry clipped the spurs on his boots, smiling at his grandfather's penchant for neatness and order.

Frank and Rolla were standing near Fan when Jerry came out, his spurs jingling with each step. Frank let out a whistle as Jerry stepped down off the porch. "Ain't you purty."

The ranch hands whistled and clapped as Jerry shoved the Winchester .22 into the scabbard hanging from his saddle. He said goodbye to each man with a handshake, then they politely disappeared. Jerry held out his hand to his grandfather. "Thank you for the spurs and the chance to do this. You believed in me even when I didn't. I want to win that bet more than anything."

"You'll do it. You just had to put some things behind you," Rolla said. "I'm hoping the world out there ain't changin' as fast as Jimmy said, but I expect you'll let us know." He let go of Jerry's hand and ambled off toward the barns. When it came to saying goodbye, Jerry knew it would be brief.

Frank stood by, watching the others. When Rolla walked away he stepped forward. "Wish I was goin' with you."

"I know. I do, too."

"I never seen California."

"I'll send some pictures when I get there."

"One of the ocean'd be nice."

"Look for it in the mail, long about the end of June."

Frank shook Jerry's hand and stared up at him with a wistful expression. It seemed he had something else to say, but he remained silent. Jerry spoke instead. "Don't worry about me, Frank. I remember everything you taught me. My back's doing better and Fan is the best horse in Oklahoma."

"Guess that's about it then. Except this." Frank removed one of the Colt .45s from his holster and handed it to Jerry. "I been usin' this six-shooter since Judge Parker over at Fort

Smith made me a deputy marshal. Them varmints that killed my father saw the smokin' end of this gun – last thing they ever did see. It shoots straight and true and I want you to have it. It's a lot better 'n that thing you're packin'."

Jerry started to protest; Frank interrupted. "And I'm gonna tell you what old Mose Beaman told me: never aim your gun at anythin' but what you want to kill, and – "

"I know," Jerry grinned, "fill your hand, you sonofabitch," they said in unison.

Frank chuckled. "Well, I'll be dawg, you have been listening."

"I don't know what to say, Frank." Frank was never without both of his six-shooters. One of his favorite sayings – "I'd rather have a pocket full of rocks than an empty gun" – Jerry had heard a hundred times. Frank had carried this Colt since he was seventeen years old. It had six notches in it. He held out his hand for Jerry's gun. Jerry handed it to him and holstered the Colt. "Thanks seems pretty slim, but I'm going to say it anyway. Thank you for everything, Frank. For Fan, for the gun, for teaching me. Don't worry, none of it went to waste. And I'll be able to tell some tales of my own when I get back."

Frank chuckled softly. "It's about time we got some new stories." He turned and walked toward the barns. Jerry swung into the saddle, turned Fan around, and set her out at a trot. When they reached the gate of the Bar R he looked back over his shoulder. Rolla, hands on his hips, stood silhouetted against the light of the open barn door, with Frank at his side. Frank had pushed his giant cowboy hat back from his forehead. They waved. Jerry touched the brim of his Stetson and headed Fan south toward Guthrie. He would spend tomorrow with his mom, dad, and brothers, and leave for California early the following day.

Jerry arrived in Guthrie at five in the afternoon and found Vearl, Edna, and Byron in the yard talking to someone. A man with a camera in his hand stood leaning against an old, dusty, black Ford. Byron came running up to Jerry, his eyes wide with excitement. "Jerry! A reporter from *The Guthrie Daily Leader* — "

"Why's he here?" Jerry asked as he rode in.

"He heard about your ride. You're gonna be in the newspaper!" Byron shouted. Jerry brought Fan to a halt a few feet away from the group.

"I'd like to get a picture," the reporter said as he aimed his camera. "So, you're riding Fancy all the way to Hollywood on a bet, are you?"

Jerry smiled at the comment just as the reporter snapped the picture. "Her name is Fan and that's exactly what I'm going to do."

# 7

## Call Collect Anytime

*The Guthrie Daily Leader*, May 4, 1946 // Jerry Van Meter and Fan Have Eye on Hollywood // Ben McGriff, Guthrie Negro, Found Guilty of Manslaughter // General Bradley's Plane Delivers Iron Lung to Muskogee for Texas Veteran

Jerry made the most of his short visit in Guthrie. He rechecked his supplies, spent time with each of his three brothers, and went over his route with his mother and father. Vearl relented and took part in the discussion this time. Jerry hardly slept that night. Saturday morning arrived with the sun hiding behind low clouds; he stepped outside. A heavy mist hung over the garden and trees as Jerry headed toward the old log barn. Inside, dressed and trail-ready Byron greeted him with, "I'm going." His pony stood saddled, a bedroll and knapsack slung over his rump.

"We talked about this, remember? Mom said you couldn't go. You've got school to finish, Byron. Besides, this might end up being a rough trip."

"Puleese, Jerry, I'll be good. I won't be any trouble. I got plenty of peanut butter and jelly." Byron's chin stuck out at a defiant angle though his eyes were holding back tears.

"I wish you could go, cowboy, but you can't. Let's ask Mom to let you ride a little way with me. We can pretend, okay?" They led their horses out into the yard. Edna emerged out the back door, wearing an apron over her wash dress.

"And where do you think you are going, Byron Van Meter?"

At the sound of her tone Byron released his unshed tears. "Please, Mom, I want to go with Jerry. Why can't – "

"Can Byron ride as far as the Eggleston place with me?" Jerry said. "It'll give us a chance to talk, and I'll make him promise to ride straight back."

Edna came forward and kissed Jerry on the cheek. "Please be careful, son. Call collect anytime and write for sure, hear?" She put her arms atop Byron's shoulders. "All right, young man. I'm trusting you to keep your word. Not another inch farther than the Eggleston place, then you turn around and come right home. Promise?"

Byron hung his head. "Promise," he said softly.

David and Bill came out of the house, pulling on their shirts, followed by a worried-looking Vearl. They exchanged quick good-byes, then Jerry and Byron mounted their horses and galloped away, waving their hats like the movie cowboys they loved.

"Yahoo," Byron hollered as soon as they were out of earshot.

His little brother rode three miles with Jerry, all the while pretending they were running from outlaws. He kept up a stream of pretend chatter, then became quiet as they reached the edge of their neighbor's ranch.

"Okay, Byron, this is as far as you go. I want you to ride straight home. I'll send a card on the trip, a special one just for you. Okay?" Jerry and Byron hugged awkwardly atop their horses and then Jerry turned Fan and trotted off. A short distance away he looked back. Byron was staring after him, tears streaming down his face. Jerry reined Fan to a halt, turned her around and waved his hat like they always did. He waited. Byron stood up in his stirrups and waved back, his good-bye lost in the distance and his tears.

"Bye, cowboy," Jerry called out. He turned Fan and whacked her on the rump with his hat. He dared not look back. Jerry rode hard until he and Fan were well away from the Eggleston Ranch.

When the early fog dissipated the dazzling prairie sun hung high in the sky. West and south of Guthrie lush green wheat fields covered the landscape, broken only by stands of cottonwood, jack pine, and elm. A breeze rolled over the top of the wheat, creating rippling waves of light and dark green. Jerry passed red dirt roads that crooked their way through the fields to clapboard houses where irises bloomed in profusion. Rusty farm equipment sat not far from clotheslines with overalls, work shirts, and bed sheets blown stiff in the wind.

Jerry crossed the Snake, the Cox, and the Pawnee Creeks that ran full, each lined by a dense thicket of trees. Fat, shiny horses grazed in huge pastures dotted with Herefords and lanky Longhorns. He encountered an occasional fence, usually barbed wire stapled to wooden posts. Jerry used his Finch pliers to pull the staples out from three or four posts, to offer slack for Fan to safely pass, then he tacked the wires back in place. In the distance the occasional grain silos rose from the horizon like rural skyscrapers.

"Do you feel like we're on a vacation, Fan?" She wanted to run but Jerry held her to a jog and lope gait, trying to pace the frisky mare. He had to average a minimum of thirty miles every day to win the bet. *Whatever the bet is*, he thought.

He'd never known his grandfather to gamble. And from the stories Jerry had heard, Charlie Goodnight adamantly opposed gambling, even forbidding his trailhands to play poker. He once fired three of his four wranglers on a cattle drive because he'd caught them gambling after he had twice warned them. Charlie's action left only himself and one other man to drive two thousand head of cattle. Principle mattered to Charlie Goodnight.

Jerry was three years old in 1929 when Charlie Goodnight passed away. Though they had never met, he felt a kinship with the man. Rolla and Frank had told stories about Charlie for as long as he could remember. Rolla admired him, called him Uncle Charlie as a term of respect (though they were cousins a couple of times removed). Both men were self-educated, tireless, charismatic, independent – they epitomized the pioneer spirit and they were protective of their way of life. That Rolla had made a bet with Jimmy Wakely in the first place, and a bet that would take Jerry from his chores at the Bar R for several months in the second place, did not fit his grandfather's character. But Rolla *had* made the bet. That fact spoke volumes to Jerry about the importance of this ride.

After three days out, Jerry and Fan reached Clinton, Oklahoma, and made their nightly camp near Route 66. They crossed the highway – empty at that moment – and paused at its edge to look east and west. It stretched across the flat landscape into infinity, a ribbon of promise that had transported countless Okies west in their flivvers and Model Ts and every other means of transportation. Piled high with kids and possessions, sometimes with chickens and farm animals thrown in, Okies had run from blinding dust and grinding poverty to California. As long as Jerry could remember everyone called California the "land of milk and honey." Now it was his destination.

Jerry and Fan arrived at the Mother Road at supper time. He made camp on the south side, away from the highway. Cars went by, silently from his distance, their headlights arcing flashes of color in the disappearing light. A steady stream of big trucks thundered past. The breeze lofted the whine of their cranked-up diesel engines over his camp, then the sound quickly disappeared, gobbled up by the forever-landscape. In the intervals between the cars and trucks Jerry heard the familiar sounds of crickets, chattering ground squirrels, and later the yip-yip-yip of coyotes in the distance.

Jerry's pot beans tasted bland compared to the ones Frank and Rolla made, and his sourdough biscuits got slightly burned on the bottom. But he washed everything down with strong coffee and promised himself his cooking would get better. After supper Jerry sat by his campfire watching the lights race past, imagining movie stars, palm-lined boulevards, and miles of sandy beaches, and wondering what adventures awaited him.

36

# OKLAHOMA

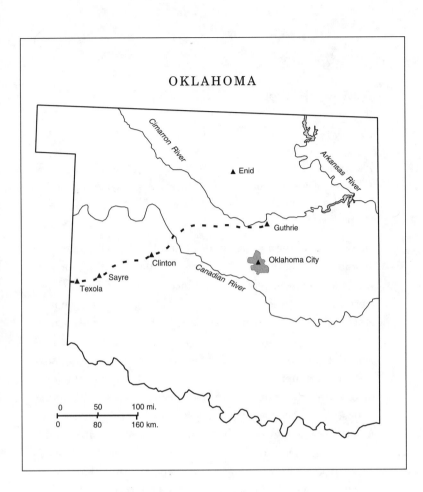

# 8

## A Mean Place

*The Amarillo Globe News*, May 8, 1946 // Truman Wants Traffic Rules Tightened to Prevent "Nuts & Morons" from Buying Licenses // Amarillo Man's Essay Wins Him a Flying Fortress B-17 // Showers, Thunderstorms, Frost Due

On day five of their journey, Jerry and Fan left Oklahoma at Texola and rode into the Texas panhandle. The difference in the landscape was at once magnificent and terrifying. Gone were the color green and the gently rolling hills of his home state; gone was any gentleness at all. The panhandle opened into a vastness that dwarfed anything he could have envisioned. Up close it appeared unforgiving and threatening, the terrain interrupted only by a rare wash or draw. Stretched out before him the sight sent a thrill through Jerry – the land's majesty and the sheer endlessness of it. Not fettered by normal, life-giving growth, the landscape sprouted occasional scrub brush, scrawny cottonwoods, mesquite and cacti, and greasewood trees whose acrid odor repelled animal and man alike. Thunderheads boomed above and rain-filled clouds scutted across the sky, driven by a booming wind that Jerry was to learn was the defining characteristic of this land of extremes. He used his Finch pliers to undo the intermittent barbed wire fences they encountered. After Fan crossed he always tacked it back like he had found it.

For the next two days he and Fan could not escape the blowing sand. Swept from the earth as if Mother Nature were sweeping her floor, the wind flung it at them, stinging Jerry's eyes, scouring his face, his hands, anything exposed. He put his red kerchief up over his nose and mouth, but even with them covered he could feel the dirt invade his lungs. Sand coated the both of them from head to foot, collecting around Fan's nostrils and forelock and forming muddy rivulets in the creases of Jerry's clothes. He remembered seeing pictures of the duststorms of the thirties, of dead horses and cows lying in the dirt, choked by lack of water and overcome by dust when Oklahoma's topsoil blew out of the state on hurricane-force winds.

Jerry found a campsite at the bottom of a shallow draw where if he hunkered down, the dirt blew over his head. He felt lucky to find any respite from the conditions. Scrawny cottonwoods lined the shallow ditch, their twisted exposed roots snaking down into the streambed in search of moisture. Their tenacious leaves and wind-scarred trunks and branches formed a meager shield from the wind's effects, but Jerry said a silent thank you for them. He tethered Fan close to the trees, washed her face and around her eyes with water from his canteen, and covered her with her blanket. He fed Fan first, stroking her neck and offering words of encouragement. She ate with her rump turned toward the wind, ears laid down in a picture of misery and irritation.

Jerry had to deal with his own brand of suffering that was unrelated to the hostile elements. A vast, all-encompassing silence surrounded him, an unrelenting and formidable enemy, something he hadn't counted on or given a thought to when planning the trip. Boundless space and open country, a silence so intense it made him catch his breath once he became aware of it on their second day out. They had been gone seven days, this their third night in Texas. Each new day brought incredible vistas, excitement, and wonder. But as each day unfolded hour by hour, the quiet chased him like a predator following its prey. Jerry felt a yawning solitude, an awareness of how small and alone he was in the vastness that surrounded him.

The wind-driven rain arrived, turning the layer of dirt on Jerry's clothes to mud. Though it added to their discomfort,

39

Jerry welcomed it. He spread his bedroll on the west side of the bank and unrolled one of his chaps to cover his face. Wind and rainstorm aside, he slept as soon as he closed his eyes.

Bright sunshine greeted him the next morning, and along with it the wind. Overnight it had abated only slightly. Frozen puddles in the shady bottom of the draw were the only evidence of the night's rain. A freshness on the dry earth was all that was left behind from what had fallen over the desert plain.

Contrary to her usual demeanor, Fan was still disconsolate when he watered and fed her. Her personality had emerged with each passing day. She loved to be scratched under the chin and always stretched her neck for more. She loved apples but would also eat cookies if they were offered; she preferred rolled oats over bran – ground oats and wheat – and she liked Timothy hay better than the grass or alfalfa variety.

But this morning, in the middle of the Texas panhandle, Fan had no intention of wearing a saddle. She flattened her ears and bared her big yellow teeth, backed up, sidestepped, and did everything she could to keep the saddle off. Using the trees to restrict her movement, Jerry held her reins taut with his left hand and hoisted the saddle up and onto her back with his right – a difficult maneuver even for a strong cowhand. Despite the morning's cold, sweat popped out on his forehead from the effort. "Dammitall, Fan, what's the matter with you? We gotta do this together."

Once he had secured the saddle, she seemed resigned and stood quietly, watching him expectantly. Jerry bent over to retrieve his bedroll and chaps just as a gust of wind whipped over them. Off came his Stetson; the wind sent it tumbling along the ground. Before he could run after it, Fan trotted over and picked it up. Jerry stood open-mouthed and watched her walk back and stop in front of him, his hat hanging from her mouth. Jerry's chuckle turned into a belly laugh that shook him until tears ran down his face. Like a big overgrown pup covered with dirt, Fan stood staring at him with innocent brown eyes, offering up not a stick or a ball, but one slightly slobbered-on Stetson. Jerry took his hat from her, wiped it off and placed it on his head.

"Nobody's *ever* gonna believe this, most of all Frank and Grandpa. I can't believe it myself," he said, wiping his eyes with the back of his hand. "If you're trying to make up for being stubborn, you picked a damned memorable way to do it." Jerry was still smiling as they headed off, the silence temporarily forgotten.

Despite the miserable conditions, they were ahead of schedule. Eight days out and they had covered two hundred fifty-five miles.

Jerry stopped for supplies at a store on Sixth Street in the San Jacinto area of Amarillo, just off Route 66. Amarillo looked like a booming town. Shiny cars whizzed by them then headed off down streets lined with stately cedars, green lawns, and big brick homes. Well-dressed men and women walked along the sidewalks, while children hopscotched ahead of them. The parents smiled; the children stopped their games and waved as Jerry and Fan rode past.

He felt embarrassed by his appearance. Trail dirt covered his clothes, and though he had shaved and washed his face, he could only hope it was dirt free. His shaving mirror fit into the palm of his hand and reflected only tiny round fragments of his face. Jerry opened the door of San Jacinto Mercantile to find the prettiest girl he'd ever seen.

Other customers gave Jerry a quick curious glance, but the pretty girl didn't seem put off by his dirt-covered clothes. When he answered "Hollywood" to her question of where he was headed, she flirted openly, asking if he was going there to be a movie star.

"Not even close." He smiled.

She introduced herself, Claire Elizabeth Dupree, announcing her name in a soft smooth voice and drawing out "Dupreeee" in a sweet Texas drawl that raised the hair on the back of Jerry's neck. Slender and petite with creamy white skin and bright red lipstick, Claire Elizabeth wore her cornsilk blond hair rolled into a perfect pompadour. And pretty Claire Elizabeth Dupree, who said her daddy owned the store, smelled of lavender perfume that filled the air and made Jerry take a deep breath. She rang up his groceries slowly, turning each can deliberately to find a price, weighing the individual pieces of fruit, and wrapping each egg separately in butcher paper. Claire kept up a steady stream of conversation as she asked about his trip, listening attentively to his every word. Jerry nodded and answered and watched, enthralled by her interest, mesmerized by her voice and graceful hands. A loud whap yanked him out of his trance; the wind had slammed a metal sign over on its side in front of the store. A customer raced past the window, chasing after his hat that the wind had stolen.

"My gosh, look at that," Jerry said. Fan jumped at the noise. Tethered securely she pranced her hind quarters from side to side. "I've got to get my horse out of that wind." Jerry retrieved his wallet from a back pocket. "And I better hurry before she kicks somebody."

"It can get a lot worse. When it really gets ripping we've had big trucks blow right over on their sides," Claire Elizabeth said. "Sometimes it quiets down after dark, then again it might howl all night long."

"Thanks, I'll remember that." Jerry paid ninety-five cents for his purchases.

Claire Elizabeth offered her hand. "Good luck, Mr. Oklahoma Cowboy. Y'all come back when you can stay longer."

Jerry reluctantly said good-bye, jammed his hat down tight, and stepped outside. He deposited his groceries into the saddlebags and threw the gunny sack filled with twenty pounds of rolled oats across Fan's rump. He headed Fan across the highway, his head still swirling with the fragrance and image of the pretty girl. They rode south for a short distance along the edge of a highway, then turned southeastward at the outskirts of the city. As soon as they returned to the open plains, the image of Claire Elizabeth quickly evaporated, scoured from Jerry's mind by the elements. The afternoon sun's glare bounced off the light-colored sand and into his eyes; the wind slammed him with dirt-laden gusts. He pulled the red kerchief over his face once again and pressed on. *Damn, Claire Elizabeth Dupree, why do you have to be from such a mean place?*

The difference between Jerry's Oklahoma and this part of Texas was more than the landscape's lack of gentility. Except for Amarillo, the towns Jerry had passed were tiny, and the few people he had seen scurried from one building to another to get out of the wind. Between the towns he found nothing but the wind-swept panhandle, with the only sign of life an occasional windmill. The troughs at these windmills provided a source of water for Fan.

In contrast, the Oklahoma prairie was covered with wheat, sorghum, and broomcorn, some of it planted the new way – not in straight rows but following the contour of the hills to prevent erosion. The effect was a gentle sort of beauty. West and south of Guthrie Jerry had seen big Caterpillar graders scooping out low spots, creating farm ponds on prairie ranches. Word had it that there would eventually be two hundred thousand farm ponds all over Oklahoma. "The water supply has to be made predictable," Governor Kerr had said in a radio broadcast. Lakes and reservoirs, too, would be built.

Jerry headed Fan southeast across weed-covered sand dunes studded with yucca and prickly pear. The wind held steady. He put a hand to his ear to lessen the noise. *Total silence except Fan's breathing.* He looked around – no fences, no people, only an alert-looking prairie dog peeking at them from his hole. There was nothing but sand and endless plains. Jerry reached up to secure his Stetson and caught a whiff of

43

Claire Elizabeth's lavender perfume on his hand. The gnawing loneliness he fought to hold at bay until he could conquer it swamped him unexpectedly and out of nowhere and grabbed him in a vise that took his breath away. Jerry shook himself and looked around, then shook himself again. He tried whistling but couldn't with his mouth covered by his kerchief. He hummed instead, and silently mouthed Rolla's words: "whatever happens, you'll handle it." After two hours of riding, Jerry at last saw the welcome signs of man as they reached the northern rim of the Palo Duro Canyon. In the distance he spotted the silhouette of several buildings; it looked like a school or college campus.

The north end of the canyon was no more than a few hundred yards wide and the same in depth. The jagged, ledge-covered walls were naturally hewn of the sun's colors, becoming richer and the layers more vivid as the sun's last rays settled on them. The Palo Duro was another of Mother Nature's wondrous creations, a huge fissure in the earth that disappeared into the distance a hundred miles away. Jerry wanted to ride into it, to see and smell it for himself. This canyon had once been home to a man who, though he had never met him, had shaped what Jerry believed in and influenced the very way he lived his life.

Jerry found an old trail, and it took an hour for them to descend to the floor of the old J.A. Ranch. He could only stare. Connections clicked and stories that had been stored deep in Jerry's memory surfaced, bringing with them an acute sense of familiarity. Frank's and Rolla's words echoed in his head: "The canyon had wall-to-wall cattle, Jerry. It was a cattleman's paradise, boy. The Palo Duro ain't nothin' like you ever seen." And they were dead on. The Palo Duro was a different world from the wind-swept, barren plain above.

Between the cream, red, brown, and rust-striated sandstone walls stretched a grass range dotted with brittle red cedars, wild chinas, cottonwoods, and hackberry trees. Prairie

44

Dog Creek ran full with tiny streams jutting off from it in every direction. Leading Fan on foot, Jerry followed the tributary to the far wall, where at the caprock high above the jagged ledges, the water flowed down from a spring. He walked the width of the canyon, sometimes stopping to scoop up loose dirt, briefly smell it, and then watch it flow through his fingers. Kneeling at a stream, he washed his hands in the cold water while Fan drank. The formations, the trees, the smell of the grass, all seemed familiar. Being here was like opening the pages of one of his brother David's comic books and stepping into an enchanted land.

After Jerry picketed Fan, he built a fire. Next he led her into the icy waterfall where he washed off the sweat and sand from the both of them. Anxious to get rid of the caked-on mud, he laundered his clothes and Fan's blanket and hung them on the bare branches of a red cedar by the fire. Then he cut a supple branch from a cottonwood and rigged a fishing pole by attaching together a hook and some string he'd brought on the trip.

Soon the aroma of pan-fried trout mingled with mesquite smoke and sweet grass. Jerry whistled while he cooked. Picketed on a hundred-foot rope, Fan was busily munching her way along the length of it. He silently thanked his grandfather for making the bet, for giving him this chance to glimpse into Charlie Goodnight's world.

The Palo Duro had been the ancestral camping grounds of the Comanches. Its walls, holders of centuries of secrets, formed majestic stone formations that were more dramatic than any man could have devised. Long after the light faded Jerry sat staring up at more stars than he'd ever seen before. Stories, anecdotes, and exploits paraded before him, tales about Charlie and this famous ranch that Jerry had heard since he was old enough to remember.

Charles Goodnight discovered the Palo Duro in 1876. Already famous as a cattle raiser and trail driver, he claimed it, put a herd on it, then attracted capital from a rich Irishman, John Adair, and his wife. Mrs. Adair happened to be the daughter of a wealthy New York banker and the sister of a senator. With the Adair's money Charlie bought more cattle – fine breeding bulls and productive cows – and coined the JA brand in honor of the couple's half-million-dollar investment. Over the next few years as many as a hundred thousand head of cattle grazed these lands; and, during any one year, Charlie would easily sell thirty thousand head. At the age of twenty – exactly Jerry's age – Charlie started his first cattle business; at thirty he and Oliver Loving blazed the Goodnight-Loving trail. And it was to the Palo Duro that young Rolla Goodnight had come to learn to be a cowboy.

Rolla and Frank told Jerry about returning with Charlie to the J.A. from a cattle drive to Kansas in 1884. On their return they discovered that Quanah Parker, Chief of the Comanches, had arrived while they were away. He had brought a band of warriors, women, and children with him. When Charlie found out they were camped at the Palo Duro, he did what he always did – made a gift of a few head of cattle to Chief Parker. Frank and Rolla helped Charlie drive them to the Comanches' camp. Charlie returned to the ranch house, but the two young cowboys stayed behind and spied on the celebration that followed. The Indians danced and drummed after they killed one of the steers and put it on a spit over the fire. Rolla and Frank told Jerry that sixty years later they could still hear the throbbing drums and see the warriors dancing by the fire. Jerry closed his eyes and listened. The drumbeat was silent. *Maybe they sat right here, around a fire just like this.*

Loneliness did not come this night, and the silence went unnoticed. Jerry felt a sense of purpose, of well-being. He was part of this place and its history, destined to be here. And Charles Goodnight was here as surely as Jerry was, sharing the warmth of his fire.

The next morning even Fan seemed to be in a good mood. She had eaten a good part of the circle during the night.

46

"Frank was right about you. Wonder if they can see that from an airplane?" Jerry said.

They rode farther into the canyon, exploring eastward until they discovered where the high-walled gorge changed to a wider expanse. An endless natural range enclosed by its own sandstone bluffs, the J.A. was a cattle rancher's dream. And like the man who had once owned it, the Palo Duro was an anomaly – heaven compared to the hostile plains above. It felt like home, and Jerry hated to leave.

After a steep climb, they reached the western rim of the canyon at noon. Jerry dismounted and glanced over his map and notes while Fan cooled down. He took a last look eastward as the straight-up sun sent shafts of light down into the depths. "You're part of the reason I'm here, Charlie, this Goodnight tradition and proving I'm part of it," he said softly.

Only the wind answered him. Jerry turned Fan away from the Palo Duro and headed toward New Mexico.

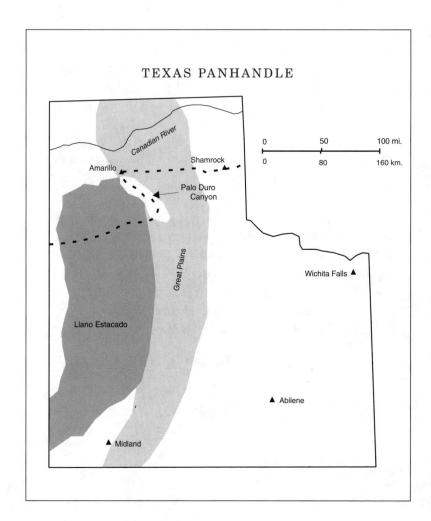

TEXAS PANHANDLE

Canadian River

Shamrock

Amarillo

Palo Duro
Canyon

Great Plains

Wichita Falls ▲

Llano Estacado

▲ Abilene

▲ Midland

| 0 | 50 | 100 mi. |
| 0 | 80 | 160 km. |

# The Llano Estacado

*Clovis News Journal*, May 14, 1946 // Candidate for Governor Arrested // Neighboring Quay County Wheat Crop a Failure // Annual Salvation Army Drive Goal, $9,700 // Dow Jones Average Hits 191

Jerry and Fan approached the outskirts of Clovis, New Mexico, on the Texas border, after two days of riding cross-country. From the looks of it, spring on the Llano Estacado – the common name for New Mexico's high plains – meant thunderstorms. Huge black clouds blotted out the sun, and the wind had a chill to it. Gusting from the northwest it kicked up dust and swirled it into dust devils that danced past them then disappeared into the air. Jerry jammed his hat down and lowered his chin.

Fan worried him. She had been off her feed since the day they left the Palo Duro. That same night Jerry noticed pimple-looking bumps on her back. Over the past two days she had become increasingly lethargic and now she had a runny nose. Her breathing seemed labored. Distemper produced those kinds of symptoms; he knew he'd better get her to a vet and fast. Jerry glanced up at the sky, suddenly aware that the storm was going to come first, like it or not.

With no warning, Fan stopped. Jerry took his worried gaze off the sky and dismounted. Strings of mucus poured from her nose; she was wheezing, and her head was hanging down almost to the ground. His heart pounded as he placed a hand on Fan's neck to see if she had a fever. "My God, Fan, you're in bad shape and getting worse by the minute. You need help." Lightning streaked through the black sky and thunder crashed on its heels. They needed shelter even more than they needed help. And, like a prayer answered, Jerry spotted the first buildings he'd seen in two days. "Come on girl, we've got to make a run for it."

Jerry started trotting, pulling Fan by her lead rope. She followed reluctantly, needing constant urging to keep moving. As Jerry drew closer he could see that the structure closest to the road was a barn. Its doors opened, and a man just inside motioned them in. Lightning and thunder crashed above them simultaneously; rain let loose in a cloudburst, and Jerry sprinted the last ten yards with Fan now leading the way.

"This looks like a doozy even by Clovis standards," the man shouted above the storm. "You and your mare better wait this one out inside."

Jerry wiped his face on his sleeve. "Thanks, mister," he shouted back. "Snot's pouring out of my horse's nose. I'm afraid it's distemper."

"Full-blown, I'd say."

"I don't want to infect your animals."

The man waved off Jerry's concern. "I couldn't let you be out in this storm. I've got a stall away from the others. I'll call my vet. As soon as this blows over you'd best get her into town."

A clap of thunder drowned out the rest of his words. He motioned for Jerry to follow him. Three horses pranced nervously in their stalls and whinnied as the storm intensified. Jerry followed the rancher to a single stall at the opposite end of the barn away from the open door. The enclosure had fresh straw covering the floor. The rancher helped Jerry get Fan inside. "I really appreciate this," Jerry said. I'll be sure to clean the stall out before we leave."

"That's okay, son. You've got a pretty sick mare. Soon as you can, you'd better get her to Doc Rivers's place. It's off this road." He indicated the road that ran alongside his property. "I'll have my son burn the straw and wash the bucket out with lye. It's nothing we haven't done plenty of times before."

Jerry removed Fan's saddle and dried her down, then put her blanket back on. She stood listless with her head lowered and eyes half-closed. The rancher brought a bucket of water and Fan drank a small amount but refused the bran and hay he offered. He told Jerry to make himself at home and then sprinted out through the rain to his house to call the vet.

"Don't worry, girl, I'm going to get you some help soon as I can." Jerry bent close and spoke in a calm, reassuring voice. He cupped his hand and applied gentle pressure back and forth along the crest of Fan's neck, something she liked as much as she liked being scratched under her chin. She rewarded Jerry with a soft nicker as the thunder crashed directly above them.

The storm raged for two hours and then rumbled off over Texas. Bright sun took over the afternoon sky, bringing warmth that brought the barn's odors to life: hay, horse dung, and whiffs of damp earth. The rancher came back and opened the barn door. "Doc Rivers is expecting you," he said. Jerry thanked him for his kindness. Leading Fan, he walked the two miles into Clovis.

Jerry remembered hearing that the Llano Estacado, or "staked plains" country, had been so named because in the early days of settlement there were no trees, no rocks, nothing to mark a traveler's way. Inventive travelers drove stakes into the ground to keep from getting lost. Now, large wheat fields, beaten down by the downpour, stretched into the distance on both sides of the road.

At the edge of Clovis Jerry encountered a neatly trimmed yard with a sign, "James Rivers, DVM." The vet's office, in a barn adjacent to a white clapboard house, had a horseshoe nailed above the door. Doc Rivers came out of his house with a slap of the screen door when Jerry led Fan into the yard. "Woody called me," he said as he shook Jerry's hand. "He said you'd be bringing in your mare soon as the storm blew over. Looks like distemper all right."

The vet examined Fan thoroughly, first listening to her heart and lungs with his stethoscope and then pressing it against her side to listen to her belly. He ran his hands over her flanks and timed her pulse with his watch by pressing his finger behind Fan's left elbow. "Pulse is a little fast. She's got a fever all right." He checked her legs all the way down and then looked at her hooves. "Needs her shoes replaced," he said matter of factly. Fan didn't fight Doc Rivers when he pulled down her lower jaw and shined a light down her throat. "You are a sick girl, aren't you?" He stroked her muzzle.

Doc Rivers counted out ten large pills. "These are a sulfa-based antibiotic." He opened Fan's mouth and flipped in a pill, then placed his left palm over her nostrils as he stroked the underside of her chin with his right hand. Done in one fast, fluid motion, the trick worked: Fan jerked her head upward and the pill went right down. "Good girl," he said and repeated the procedure with a second pill. "As bad as she is, I gave her two pills to hit it hard. You give her one a day, starting this time tomorrow until they're gone." He held up a bucket of water for Fan to drink. "I'm pretty sure we got it in time, but she's one step away from pneumonia, and I don't need to tell you what that means."

Jerry told him about their journey.

"From the size of her legs and chest, I'd guess this mare is an Indian pony, a good strong horse. I think she can probably handle the trip if you rest her up – two days at least. She needs a chance for the medicine to get into her bloodstream and start working, about forty-eight hours. Once it does you can ride her, but be cautious. Rest her as often as you can."

Jerry paid the bill, and the veterinarian directed him to the Curry County Fairgrounds. "There's only a caretaker there right now, getting things ready for Pioneer Days, but you'll find some enclosed stalls." As he said good-bye the doctor made Jerry promise that if Fan still had any of the symptoms in two days he would bring her back, no charge. Jerry promised he would.

Jerry had no trouble finding the fairgrounds, a sprawling complex on the southern edge of Clovis. Adjacent to a giant

Santa Fe rail yard and some adjoining cattle pens, the fair-grounds appeared deserted. With the sun now below the horizon it had turned cold; Jerry could see his breath in the evening air. Jerry guessed that the caretaker had already gone home but he could see evidence that someone had recently been there. A bale of straw had been placed in front of each stable door. Jerry led Fan into a stall at the end of a long building, hauled the straw inside, and spread it over the floor. He found a bucket and brought in water. Fan drank a little and then lowered herself down on the straw. Fan never slept lying down. Jerry's heart sank watching her. He knelt down and stroked her neck.

"Don't die on me, girl. Please don't die," he whispered.

Jerry felt too tired to pace and too upset and frightened to sleep. He had seen injured and sick horses put down and he wanted no part of that for his valiant mare. He spread his bedroll in the corner of the stall, opened a can of pork and beans, and ate in the waning light, never taking his eyes off his exhausted horse. Later, he stretched out with his head propped against Fan's saddle. The night grew dark as Jerry lay with his eyes open, a sick dread creeping over him. Unable to drown out the sound of Fan's labored breathing, he could hear in the background the lonesome whine of train whistles. In the distance he heard cattle lowing and, farther away still, he thought he heard the sound of church bells.

# 10

## In the Nick of Time

*Clovis News Journal*, May 15, 1946 // French Prime Minister Pompidou Succeeds De Gaulle // U of Michigan Cooperates with Johns Hopkins to Build Synchroton, 300 Million Volt Current Produces Energy // Deadlocked Coal Negotiations Idle 71,000

Morning brought a slight improvement in the horse. Fan struggled to her feet, and Jerry could see that the mucus drainage had decreased. She still wouldn't eat but she drank two buckets of water. Doc Rivers had said not to worry whether she ate anything for the first twenty-four hours, that drinking water was more important than eating any food. After she drank, Fan looked at Jerry with soulful eyes, half closed them, and went back to sleep, this time standing up. He leaned his forehead against her warm side and ran his hand over her neck. "One of those damned troughs on the other side of Amarillo must have been infected. I promise you, girl, we're not leaving until you're better. I don't want to lose you, bet or no bet."

Jerry heard a knock on the stall door. Ernie, caretaker for the Curry County Fairgrounds, noticed the outside bale of hay gone and wanted to know about the fair's first guests. "We're not here for the fair. My mare came down with distemper and Doc Rivers suggested I bring her here to the fairgrounds to recuperate." Jerry told him about the trip they were on and offered to pay for the straw. His host was as hospitable as the rancher had been and would not take Jerry's money. By the looks of his bowed legs, sweat-stained Stetson, and show of concern for Fan, Jerry knew he was a cowboy; Ernie insisted on staying with her so Jerry could go in to Clovis to get supplies. "First let me get her some hay." Ernie returned in a few minutes, balancing a bale on his shoulder.

Fan never ceased to amaze Jerry. She had always been unflappable, a steady horse. Still, as sick as she was, she surprised him by not shying or backing away when Ernie came into her stall. He crooned to her in Spanish, first holding out his hand for her to smell and then moving slowly around her stall. He offered a handful of hay. "Try a little of this, chiquita mia," he said softly in a sing-song voice. A triumphant smile appeared on his leathery face when Fan began to nibble. "All the ladies love me."

"Well, this one sure does," Jerry said.

Jerry walked into town, stopping on the way to buy a copy of the *Clovis News Journal*. He easily found the restaurant that Ernie had said was frequented by local cowboys. Jerry read the paper while he waited for his breakfast. He had hardly slept since the Palo Duro and the previous night had only eaten a can of cold beans. Hungry, sleepy, and worried, Jerry silently tried to regroup as he drank his coffee, telling himself that it wasn't his fault that Fan got sick but admitting he felt guilty that she had.

Being around other people – the rancher, Doctor Rivers, Ernie, and the friendly waitress who kept bringing him coffee – helped his spirits. Jerry thought wistfully of Claire Elizabeth Dupree, her pretty smile and how good she smelled. Her image evaporated when the waitress delivered a platter of flapjacks, eggs, and bacon, the sweet aroma of lavender quickly replaced by the hearty breakfast. Jerry glanced around as he ate.

Ernie had called it right about the restaurant being a cowboy hangout. Most of the customers looked and sounded like cowhands. Jerry overheard stories and jokes about cowboys; they talked about hay crops and horses. They nodded or tipped their hats in his direction as they filed by his booth. They recognized a cowboy when they saw one. Jerry was from Oklahoma; they were from New Mexico, but the location didn't matter. They were a fraternity, these lanky, jeans-clad, boot-wearing, weathered men who called themselves cowboys. They shared a way of life, a love of horses, a respect for the land, and what they did for a living. They worried and talked about the same things Jerry talked about with his ranch hands. He didn't know their names yet he felt he was one of them. Their presence, hearing snatches of their conversation, improved his disposition as much as the food did. Jerry ate every morsel on his plate and paid the bill. He touched the brim of his hat, and each cowboy acknowledged him in return as he exited. Jerry took off through the streets of Clovis in search of a store.

The tracks of the Santa Fe rail yards separated the Curry County Fairgrounds from town. From the rail yard came a cacophony of sounds: train engines stopping and starting, iron wheels grinding against metal rails, screeches, train whistles, and clanging bells. The cattle pens flooded the air with familiar sounds and smells. The combination of sounds had helped keep Jerry awake the previous night. That, and his overwhelming concern for Fan.

Downtown Clovis was ablaze with red, white, and blue banners. Draped across Main Street they announced the upcoming festivities: "Clovis Pioneer Days June 6–8, Curry County Fairgrounds," "Big Rodeo," "Barrel Racing," "Tractor Pull," "Chili Cook-Off," "Pie Eating Contest."

Clovis was a small city with a busy downtown section surrounded by tree-lined streets and well-kept houses and yards. And, on almost every corner, a church. On the hour the town became a symphony of ringing bells, blending into a joyful melody from wooden, adobe, and brick towers. Jerry's spirits soared at the clear, pure sounds – a chorus that seemed to say things were going to be okay; Fan had gotten help in the nick of time.

Signs of an upcoming celebration – cowboys smiling and nodding their friendly hellos – made Jerry think of Enid and the Cherokee Strip celebration. He had accompanied Rolla and Frank on their two-week Chisholm Trail ride to commemorate Jesse Chisholm's founding of the cattle route. The ride ended in Enid, and their arrival signaled the beginning of the annual festivities. Those thoughts led to home and to family. It was Tuesday morning. At three p.m. the tower bell at Pleasant Valley School near Guthrie would ring, and Byron, Bill, and David would rush home to do their chores and then probably go fishing. Jerry wondered what his mom would be cooking for supper. On Sundays she cooked fried chicken. Sunday supper was *always* fried chicken. Frank and Rolla had probably been there last Sunday. Frank would surely be staying at the Bar R, helping Rolla with the summer work in Jerry's absence.

But you never knew about Frank Eaton; he never planned anything. Instead, he invited into his life whatever came his way. He always said, "If you don't make a bunch of plans, life'll be full of surprises." Rolla Goodnight maintained there wasn't another human being like Frank Eaton and he was right. The very thought of the small, wiry man made Jerry smile. Though he was close to his family in Perkins, he and Rolla were never far apart, riding together at the head of parades all through Oklahoma. In the early thirties Frank had helped build the chicken house at the Guthrie place. Frank gave David his first chew of tobacco (which made him sick) and he gave Jimmy an Indian bow he'd made from orange tree wood. Frank was a gunslinger in the finest tradition and would give you the shirt off his back or the horse out from under him. Generous, impulsive, and fearless, Frank epitomized the gun-toting, fun-loving, storytelling American cowboy. Jerry never tired of hearing his tale about shooting it out with horse thieves that were making off with Owens Cattle Company cattle, killing three of them and taking three bullets in the melee. Frank showed him the scars. "Laid me up for a while." Varmints, thieves, judges, and lawmen – Frank's stories were

57

the stuff of legends and they were true. Like Rolla, Frank loved to recount their adventures with gusto but he was honest to a fault.

Jerry bought supplies for himself, rolled oats for Fan, and two more horseshoes to use with the two he brought along. He found the Clovis Post Office at Fourth and Mitchell and went in. Jerry knew if his family didn't receive word from him soon they would get worried. Inside the building a huge mural depicting men and women hard at work on a variety of WPA projects occupied one wall. Jerry studied it as he waited in line to buy penny postcards. Lots of folks had praised Franklin Roosevelt's Works Progress Administration for the relief it offered during the Great Depression. Rolla had strong opinions about that and politics in general and would voice them at the slightest provocation.

A life-long Democrat, Rolla parted company with the Democratic president over acreage control on wheat and cotton land. He lambasted Roosevelt at every opportunity over the controls, and anyone within Rolla's earshot soon found it wise to avoid the subject altogether. Jerry smiled as he pictured the time his grandfather, brandishing his Winchester, had chased an inspector with the U.S. Department of Agriculture off the Bar R. "You may be from the U.S. Government, mister," he bellowed at the retreating figure, "but you're on U.S. Goodnight property. Now git."

Jerry arrived back at the fairgrounds in time to give Fan her pill. Ernie said she'd finally eaten a good amount of hay and offered again to watch her anytime Jerry needed to go to town. Looping the lead rope around Fan's neck Jerry led her out of the stall into the warm sun. She lifted her head and sniffed the air. The pills were taking hold; Fan looked better and seemed perkier. Jerry cleaned and trimmed her hooves and replaced all four of Fan's worn shoes.

Her underlying Osage Indian sturdiness proved itself. She bounced back quickly with two-and-a-half days of solid rest, lots of rolled oats, her favorite brand of hay, and good clean water. Jerry gave her the medicine faithfully and led her for a walk around the track three times each day to keep her muscles from stiffening. On the third evening he let her loose in a fenced-in paddock, and he and Ernie watched as Fan tossed her head and pranced. She trotted back and forth along the fence and then rolled in the dirt. Lowering herself down on her right side she rolled, got up and shook, and then lay down on her left side and did the same thing. She had gotten down and back up a lot easier than the night they arrived. "Now I know she's feeling better," Jerry said.

A dusty, straw-covered mess, she looked like the Fan he started out with. "You are one sorry-looking lady, and am I happy to see you that way," Jerry said. He stood close to the fence and whistled. "Watch this, Ernie." Fan trotted up and stuck her head over the fence close to Jerry's face. He blew into her nostril. Fan wiggled her muzzle and waited expectantly. Jerry did it again with predictable results. She whinnied, then raised and lowered her head in a giant affirmative nod, curling her top lip up to reveal all of her big front teeth. Ernie laughed aloud at her comic expression. She looked as though she was having a good laugh. Fan put her head close, wanting more. "She loves it when I do that." Jerry brushed her off and rode Fan bareback around the track. Her breathing sounded normal; she acted frisky; she seemed ready to go. "I promised you, girl, we'd wait until you were better. Now that you are, we have to get going. We've got a bet to win."

# 11

## The Rockies

*Clovis News Journal*, May 17, 1946 // Organ Dedicated to War Hero (Church Organ) // Railroad Workers Killed in Freak Rail Yard Accident // City Parking Meters "Take" Averages $100 Per Day

Ernie wished them luck the next morning and watched as they rode away. Jerry and Fan skirted the Santa Fe railroad yards and the nearby cattle pens and headed due west across the yucca-studded Llano Estacado – the very name made him sit tall in the saddle. Rolla and Frank had crossed the Llano Estacado; Charlie Goodnight and Oliver Loving and countless others had crossed it as well. This country had once been the stomping grounds of Billy the Kid and Butch Cassidy. It was high desert with a constant cool breeze, prickly cactus, and sage so thick its fragrance filled your senses. Jerry took in the panorama, and suddenly Rolla's reason for the trip became crystal clear, what it was he wanted Jerry to experience before it disappeared: vistas that filled the senses, miles of wide open country, sky without end. All these were important settings in his grandfather's and Frank's life. Now, as his own adventure unfolded, Jerry could easily picture Frank and Rolla as young men and know what they saw and felt.

Straight ahead two days' ride lay Fort Sumner on the banks of the Pecos River, the site of Billy the Kid's grave. Frank said to be sure to see it, that Pat Garrett, the lawman who had killed Billy, had been a good friend of his. And according to Rolla, Charlie's partner, Oliver Loving, had died at the fort in 1867 of complications from having his arm amputated. Loving desperately wanted to be buried in his beloved Texas. Charlie was with him until the end and had promised his friend that his wish would be honored. True to his word, Charlie rode back from Texas to the fort four months later and had Loving's body exhumed. With a specially built casket, a large crew of cowboys, and six big mules, he returned his partner's body to Weatherford, Texas, for a formal Masonic funeral. Charlie had relayed the story with great sadness when young Rolla had asked about a picture hanging on the living room wall at the J.A. Ranch. Now Jerry could feel himself reaching back in time, envisioning the world that once belonged to the famous cattle baron, the one that had forged the brotherhood of young Rolla Goodnight and Frank Eaton.

Jerry located Billy the Kid's gravesite near the banks of the Pecos River. The old fort had been preserved and probably looked much like it had in the days of the Kid. An adobe marker in the cemetery stood solidly as the final resting place of one of the West's most famous gunfighters and two of his friends. At the top of the marker was the word "Pals," and underneath "William H. Bonney, alias Billy the Kid, Died July, 1881." On either side stood the markers of two members of his gang: "Charlie Bowdre and Tom O'Folliard, Died Dec. 1880."

Jerry stood at the foot of the graves, hand on his Colt .45 – Frank's Colt .45 – mentally picturing the thousands of fast-draws he and Frank had practiced during the winter. How easy it had become. It must have been easy for the Kid, too. Who taught him? Did he have a Frank Eaton in his life? Frank had laughingly called him Jerry the Kid when Jerry had finally outdrawn him. Twenty-two-year-old Billy the Kid died the same year that Frank rode through here looking for a killer of his own.

Garrett was the law around Albuquerque when Frank caught up with Wyley Campsey in the New Mexico Territory in 1881. Campsey, wanted for the murder of an officer in the Indian Territory, was the last alive of the six men who had murdered Frank's father. Frank had already dispatched the other five. Garrett proved to be a good friend: after listening to

Frank's story he offered to arrest Campsey to avoid the risk of Frank being killed. Twenty-one years old at the time, Frank Eaton wore a deputy marshal badge and carried a letter of introduction from Captain Knipe of the Cattlemen's Association. Frank told Garrett he didn't want Campsey arrested, that his life's mission would never be finished until his father's last murderer was dead. "He or I will hear the cook call breakfast in hell."

With Garrett watching from outside the saloon's doors, Frank outdrew Campsey and his two bodyguards, killing all three. The last words they heard: "Fill your hand, you sonofabitch." Frank was hit in the leg and left arm, and one of his Colt .45s destroyed in the battle. After the shoot-out, Garrett helped Frank back on his horse, Bowlegs, and sent him to the home of a friend to get patched up and recuperate. Before Frank rode away, Garrett thanked him for getting rid of three bad guys and shoved a Colt .44 with an eight-inch barrel into one of Frank's empty holsters. Later the man who patched Frank up told him how lucky he was to have that particular gun; it was the one Pat Garrett had used to kill Billy the Kid.

Jerry rode four miles north into the town of Ft. Sumner where he replenished his supplies and bought a picture of Billy the Kid for Byron. In a stack of dusty books he found a tattered copy of *The Authentic Life of Billy the Kid by Pat F. Garrett* for Frank. Jerry sat on a bench in front of the post office and wrote a letter to his parents and one to Frank and Rolla. He mailed them with the book and the picture. As he rode away from Fort Sumner it occurred to Jerry that Frank hadn't mentioned his trip, only the gunfight itself. But he would have had to cross the Rockies to reach Albuquerque and Wyley Campsey. Frank hadn't crossed the Continental Divide sixty-five years ago because his trip had ended in Albuquerque. Jerry's route would take him farther south than Frank's, but he carried the same Colt and would cross the same mountains and sleep under the same stars as his mentor and friend. Frank had been twenty-one, Jerry was twenty. It gave Jerry a new perspective. Frank did it; he could surely do it, too.

After a full day's ride west of Fort Sumner the wind swept aside the high cirrus clouds, and Jerry got his first real look at the Rocky Mountains, all the way to the top. He slowed Fan, then brought her to a stop and dismounted. Jerry could only stare. Covered by sagebrush and dotted with golden prince's plume and pink desert mallow, the plains stretched into the distance, only ending where the mountains began. Occasional craggy peaks covered with snow jutted high into the turquoise sky, their sharpness interrupting the flowing silhouette of rounded heights, angular slopes, and vertical shale walls that made up the range. The Rockies filled Jerry's vision as high and as wide as he could see. This obstacle, if such a monument of nature could be called that, had sparked Jerry's initial fear about the ride. Now, alone with Fan, surrounded only by earth and sky, he viewed them with awe. "We're going to cross those, Fan. If we stacked Oklahoma's tallest mountain on top of itself it still wouldn't be that high."

He kept Fan on a due-west course, going cross-country through the upper Sacramento Mountains, part of the range that formed the spine of the Rockies. He stopped to buy grain at a small ranch he happened across; otherwise, rangy long-horns, astonishing vistas, and local wildlife were all he saw. Some coyotes, sitting on an outcropping of rocks just like old folks sitting on their front porch, watched Jerry and Fan pass. Jerry smiled. "Dad didn't want us to make this trip, Fan, but if he could see this he'd understand."

Pungent pine forests gave way to boulder-strewn valleys, only to rise again to pastures ringed by pine- and aspen-covered slopes. The color of the sky depended upon the time of day and ranged from an early-morning pale, translucent blue to a deep turquoise when the sun reached its zenith. Jerry took extra rests with Fan because of the altitude, well aware of the stress it exerted on her lungs. Instead of their usual three times per day they now stopped five. The terrain called for them to be constantly climbing, then descending, and then climbing again. Fish and game were plentiful; Jerry ate well.

He spotted a herd of wild mustangs across a valley. That same night he heard the powerful, unbeaten call of a wolf affirming his dominance. The long, wailing cry resonated so intensely throughout the still valley that it raised the hair on the back of Jerry's neck; he held his breath until it died, and all was quiet again. Early one morning he watched silently as a mule deer drank upwind from the same stream where he had washed up. And every day falcons, hawks, and eagles circled overhead, watching from their lofty vantage on the updrafts and wind currents. On their seventh day out of Clovis, Jerry arrived at a rocky escarpment jutting out of the tall pines. It offered his first panoramic look at what lay ahead.

Visible through a golden haze across the valley below loomed another range of mountains: the Continental Divide. As impressive as his first view of the Rockies, the mountains at that moment glowed with the colors of the setting sun. Below, the Rio Grande, deep in the shadows of early evening, ambled from north to south, lazily crooking its way between the two ranges – massive upheavals of Mother Earth millions of years in the making. Jerry eyed the view, envisioning more rimrock mesas, timbered hills, and mountainous country they would have to cross. "Back home, Fan, I thought I was a cowboy. I wasn't. But I'm pretty sure I will be by the time we get to Hollywood."

# 12

## The Continental Divide

*Socorro Chieftain*, May 25, 1946 // First Polio Case Shows Up in Socorro Area // 1 Million Injured, 16,000 Die Nationwide in 1945 Farm Accidents // $2M GI Loans to New Mexico Vets: Not One Default

Jerry and Fan made their way out of the Rockies alongside a stream that led down to the valley below. Once they reached the Rio Grande they turned south, traveling past newly planted fields of cantaloupes and chili peppers, one field after another of shiny-leafed young plants in rich-looking soil. Early the next morning they reached Socorro, New Mexico.

Once a mining center, it now functioned as a busy business and farming hub, sprawled along the western banks of the river. Socorro resembled a picturesque city in old Mexico, laid out in a grid pattern of streets, with stores and warehouses that bespoke of earlier boom times. The Atchison, Topeka, and Santa Fe train depot sat at one end of Manzanares Street, and a large central plaza was at the other. Jerry followed Manzanares a short distance into town and then turned Fan onto California Street. On the corner, the dark windows of Price-Lowenstein Mercantile told him it was early. Except for the Capitol Bar, a fine old stone building, California Street held a mixture of sagging adobe buildings with fancy brick eaves and worn wooden structures that long ago were no doubt considered grand.

Jerry saw few cars parked in front of the stores, but the early Socorro citizens who were out shopping stopped and stared at him with his collar-length hair, all-black clothes, and a tie-down holster with a Colt in it. As he rode his strutting pinto down California Street Jerry admitted he must have looked like an outlaw right out of a western movie, for a pretty little black-haired girl about five years old pointed at him and spoke excitedly to her mother. "Mira, Mama. Mira el bandito." She peeked out from behind her mother's skirts. He touched the brim of his hat as he reigned Fan up in front of a mercantile store whose clerk was just opening its doors.

The clerk at J. L. Grimes Store spoke very little English; Jerry spoke even less Spanish. There were no other customers, and the young señorita tried desperately to help. He searched for a tube of Ipana toothpaste but could not find one and had no idea how to ask for it. Finally Jerry mimed squeezing toothpaste onto an imaginary brush, brushing his teeth, and then ended his pantomime with a big smile.

"Ah, Señor, pasta dentífrica." After much giggling she produced the toothpaste from behind the counter; it cost twenty cents. Jerry didn't try to find Unguentine, the ointment he needed for his sun-and wind-burned face. As he exited, Jerry ran smack into the Socorro law.

"Good morning. Mind if I ask what you're doing carrying a gun?" His name was Alfredo Baca and he identified himself as chief of Socorro police. Chief Baca explained that Grimes Mercantile had been robbed twice in the last six months, as had the drugstore, the post office, and the Sprouse-Reitz store. He was more than a little curious about a shaggy-haired young man armed with a Colt riding through his town. Jerry told him about the trip they were on and presented the receipt for the groceries and feed he had just bought.

Captain Baca apologized for his interrogation and walked with Jerry back to Fan's side. "Good looking pinto," he said.

Fan strained forward as Jerry approached. She had learned by now that when he walked toward her with a gunny sack she would shortly be getting a taste of rolled oats. Jerry held the sack open; Fan stuck her nose in and began chomping.

"A good-looking and hungry pinto. Vaya con Dios, mi amigo," Captain Baca said as Jerry rode away.

Fan was eating good again. Jerry carried four to five days' supply of grain – about twenty-five pounds of protein food, an important fuel. She ate grass at every opportunity and liked the occasional hay that Jerry had been able to get for her on the trip. Still, he could tell when he tightened her cinch that Fan had lost weight. But, then, he had too; Jerry had to tighten his own belt.

Jerry followed the general direction of Highway 60 due west from Socorro. Machines and crews were busy at work on the old two-lane road at the base of the mountain. Jerry did not own a car and, even if he could have afforded the $1,125 price tag for a new one, they were as scarce as new housing. The war had consumed the country's raw materials, and according to radio and newspapers it would be two years before production would make them readily available. The word *progress* flicked through Jerry's mind.

Jerry and Fan traveled in a straight line up the eastern slopes of the Continental Divide. They seldom intersected the curving highway that ambled its way around thickly forested mountain peaks. He stopped to rest Fan in Magdalena, a village sprawled in the sun at the base of Lady Magdalena Mountain. This was cattle and sheep country, and Magdalena served as its center. Gangly cowboys, dark-skinned Indians, and a fair number of eastern tourists trying to look like westerners ambled in and out of the hotel, the post office, and the train station. Magdalena stood at the end of a spur railroad line. Railcars parked on the tracks, with their doors opened to adjoining rows of connecting pens, were being loaded, some with bawling cattle, others with sheep. It was shipment time, a time Jerry knew well.

The climb was gradual but constant, and the surroundings dramatic. From a trail that led between ten-thousand-foot forested peaks, Jerry and Fan entered the Plains of San Augustin, an ancient concave lake bed ringed in the far distance by more towering mountains. It was a wild, rugged country of

67

one spectacular vista after another. Jerry and Fan passed cattle herds being driven to the rail yard in Magdalena. The cowhands accompanying them offered a friendly wave in Jerry's direction. Sheep bunched in tight flocks as their Basque sheepherders kept them moving briskly along at a respectful distance from the longhorns. Jerry made camp near the tiny town of Datil along the southeastern rim of the plains.

Mountainside slopes that received sunlight were thick with piñons and junipers, while the shady hillsides were covered with conifers. At five the following afternoon, warm sunlight gave way to dark skies and a chill-to-the-bone wind that blew straight at them. Jerry would have liked to ride for another two hours but the threatening skies and eight-thousand-foot elevation helped him decide against it. He rode a half-mile off the highway and found a protected spot to camp.

Jerry donned his rain slicker and picketed Fan near a wall of granite boulders. A nearby grove of piñon trees would provide a canopy if it snowed, and snow looked imminent. He unpacked his gear, watered and fed Fan, and then got a fire going. As he looked around at his camp Jerry congratulated himself for his choice of sites. The wall of boulders would reflect the fire's heat and protect them from the wind. The coming storm wasn't nearly as worrisome now.

An hour of daylight remained and Jerry intended to use it to bag his dinner. Grabbing his Winchester he hiked ten minutes in a straight line due north from camp until he came to the edge of a meadow. He crouched down and waited to see what would appear. A faint honking sound high above made him look up; he saw a formation of Canada geese heading north. They were out of range but Jerry acknowledged he wouldn't have shot one anyway – to do so would have created a space in that perfect V formation. Thirty minutes went by. Jerry had almost resigned himself to eating beans when three grouse flew out of the woods and landed in the meadow. He got the first one he aimed at.

Jerry usually hunted or fished four days out of seven, even more while in the mountains where small game was plentiful. He could gut, skin, flour, and prepare any game in fifteen minutes flat, a long-ago lesson learned from his father. Jerry built a spit and spent the next hour turning the bird until it was a golden brown.

Snow started falling just as he finished his meal. Not just flurries like they'd experienced in the Rockies, but a wind-driven, blinding snow that blanketed trees and rocks and coated everything, vertical and horizontal. Within an hour four inches had fallen in camp and more could be seen out away from the rocks. The snow gave Jerry an eerie feeling, boxing him in, obscuring distance and perspective, cutting off all sound with its insulation. He knew if it snowed hard all night and the wind kept up, they would have a difficult time getting through the snowdrifts.

There hadn't been any car lights since he made camp. The only sounds were the crackling fire and the howling wind, which made Fan nervous. She was used to Oklahoma winds – which this was not – and she didn't like snow at all. Tense and fidgety, she shook her head, switched her tail abruptly, and kept shifting directions. Jerry got up and brushed the snow off her. He cupped his hand and massaged along the ridge of her neck.

"Hey, this is just a little snow. Don't worry," he crooned. His voice seemed to settle her. Jerry huddled by the fire and tried to think about the following day. His rational mind told him that Pietown was only eight miles ahead; his emotional mind insisted that he and Fan were totally alone on the mountaintop. Nervous, Jerry busied himself gathering dry wood from under low-hanging branches. He stacked it against the rocks. "I've got to make sure to wake up and keep the fire going," Jerry said in Fan's direction.

He covered his bedroll with his rain slicker and then added a few pieces of piñon to the fire. The resinous wood sizzled and spit, sending forth heat and quick spikes of flame. Knowing Fan would need water to drink in the morning he heaped snow in the bucket and placed it at the edge of the fire.

Light replaced darkness and Jerry awoke the next morning to a terrible smell. He opened his eyes with a start and gazed directly into Fan's yellow teeth. She nuzzled his cheek. "Fan." Jerry let out a startled holler. "For cryin' out loud, your breath smells awful." He jumped up and stood shivering on top of his snow-covered bedroll.

It had stopped snowing. Still, as protected as it was, his camp was buried under a foot of snow. He figured the two mounds near his bedroll had to be cowboy boots. Jerry dumped the snow out of them, pulled them on, then removed the snow from his bedroll. Everything he touched was wet and ice cold. He had a hard time finding his hat. The fire had burned out long before he awoke and the remaining wood stuck out of the snow just far enough for him to find it. Fan looked like a four-legged snowman. And the water in the bucket had a one-inch layer of solid ice on top.

"Dammitall, Fan, if you wanted to wake me, why didn't you do it in the middle of the night?" Jerry stomped out away from Fan and stood under a piñon tree, its branches loaded with snow. He looked back at his sorry camp. "Damn it all!" he roared, and threw up his arms in disgust.

The sharp sound dislodged the snow. It landed squarely on Jerry's uncovered head, forming a cone on top and creating peaks on his nose, eyelashes, and shoulders. He could hardly see. It slid down his collar and made icy streams down his back. Jerry brushed it off his face and saw Fan watching him, flicking her ears back and forth.

Now he was disgusted *and* wet. "I said dammitall!" Jerry shouted again, and shook himself. Fan whinnied. "I get the impression you think this is funny."

Maybe Fan shook her head trying to get the snow off, or perhaps her muzzle itched and that's why she wiggled it, showing

70

her big teeth. But to Jerry it looked like she was having a good laugh, a "yup, serves you right" kind of look.

"Before you go laughing at me, missy, you should see yourself. You don't look much better."

Jerry dug out his hat and rebuilt the fire. He cleaned the snow off Fan and shook out her blanket. The water in the bucket finally thawed enough to get coffee going. Fan stood with her head over his shoulder next to his face as he squatted by the fire. She wanted water. "Okay, okay, you don't want to drink ice water. Let me fix this, will you?" Fan eventually got her water and grain. Jerry ate cold biscuits dunked in hot coffee and two half-frozen eggs that he fried to unthaw.

By late morning they made their way back to the highway. The main part of the storm front had moved east. A few scattered clouds remained, blocking the sun and making the forest look cold, white, and unforgiving. Thirty minutes later the sun popped out and Jerry immediately felt its warmth. The snow-laden trees suddenly became a kaleidoscope of flashing light and color, dazzling and brilliant, like being in the midst of a sparkly Christmas card.

The top layer of snow on the highway had blown away with the wind. Fan, not sure of her footing, moved slowly through the eight inches that remained, suspicious of every step. Jerry walked ahead until she was wading through it with no hesitation. When he was satisfied that the road beneath the snow was smooth and even Jerry mounted up. The last thing he wanted was a leg injury to Fan. She walked confidently along the vacant highway through fresh powder that was halfway up her forearm.

Jerry patted Fan's neck. "The worst is over, girl. We'll be out of the snow soon. Things are going to get better now."

# 13

## Seven Thousand Feet and Climbing

*The Socorro Chieftain*, May 26, 1946 // Rotarians Hear of Freezing Food for Preservation // Magdalena Stockyards Gear Up for Cattle, Sheep, Rail Shipments // Reports of Diphtheria Cancel Datil Fiesta // Wheat Shortage Drives Bread Prices to Dime a Loaf

The constant strain of the altitude began to show on Fan. Except for the two days they'd camped along the Rio Grande, they had been above seven thousand feet and as high as ten thousand for ten days. Lathered and breathing hard, she walked with a slow, plodding step. Jerry dismounted and walked in front. He kept up a steady stream of conversation, partly to encourage Fan, partly to keep himself from worrying. "Come on, you water-guzzlin', hay-eatin' machine. We can't let this mountain lick us." Fan snorted and Jerry chuckled, certain she was letting him know she didn't appreciate his unflattering description. "Okay, okay, I take back what I said."

The day grew hot under the bright sun. A great clump of snow released from a nearby pine with a thump, startling Fan. "At least it didn't land on my head or yours." Another clump fell, and another, echoing like muted dominoes falling in the stillness. Jerry wet his lips and whistled "Cool, Clear Water," a Sons of the Pioneers song. He looked back. Fan held her head higher; she looked alert, switching her tail as though irritated. "So, I can't carry a tune." Jerry alternately whistled and talked until his mouth got too dry to do either. When they reached Pietown near the top of the Divide, Jerry paused to catch his breath and let his heartbeat slow down.

At over eight thousand feet, the thin crystalline air made getting enough oxygen difficult. But it did afford a spectacular setting; pure white snow and a forest of blue-green trees, all set against a cloudless turquoise sky. Pietown, however, had seen better days. It was nothing more than a few sad-looking buildings, and its busiest business seemed to be a ramshackle restaurant that advertised homemade pies. Jerry could see people through the fogged-up windows. In front of the building two tethered horses slept in the sun near an old buckboard with two mules hitched to it. As soon as Jerry caught his breath, he and Fan moved on, leaving Pietown behind. Three miles later they crested the Divide.

When Fan's breathing slowed he climbed back into the saddle. "Okay, girl. We'll get as far west of Quemado as daylight will allow, then I'm gonna find you a big patch of grama grass and a nice stream." The snow was melting fast, and the downslope on the west side of the Divide was gentle enough to make the going considerably easier. Jerry let Fan pick her own speed, and she chose the running walk that was responsible for her name.

Late afternoon brought them to Quemado near the western edge of the San Francisco River. The old village surrounding a tiny plaza sat in a valley two thousand feet below the summit. Three fine old buildings constructed of cut stone faced onto the highway; the other structures were adobe, made drab by a layer of gray limestone wash. The remainder of Quemado consisted of rutted dirt side streets with a few tidy houses. Most, however, were in various states of disrepair. Some streets ended in nothingness several blocks off the highway. At the end of one sat a sheetless covered wagon, its exposed rusted stays resembling the ribs of a long-dead creature.

The people looked like none Jerry had ever seen – short and dark-skinned with blue-black hair – could they be gypsies? Women dressed in once-bright layered skirts and faded blouses walked past unsmiling, leading scantily dressed children by the hand. The men, most of them wearing balloon-legged pants with wide belts and worn vests, stared back at him with open curiosity as he rode by. They didn't look like any cowboys he had ever seen.

Quemado's Country Store had to be the biggest building in town. The size of a warehouse, it had two ancient gas pumps in front. Inside, the majority of the space had been blocked off, leaving only a small front section for the dusty, cluttered collection of goods. Grimy windows let in little of the bright sun outside. The store smelled of grain, coal oil, and sweaty unwashed bodies. The minute he walked in, Jerry experienced a disquieting feeling. Several customers glanced his way; none acknowledged him. Jerry noticed immediately that the gypsy-looking people spoke a language different than Spanish. And no one spoke English.

Buying supplies on the trip had been something Jerry usually enjoyed. It gave him a chance to visit with people and learn about the area, even if his host turned out to be the local sheriff. These people eyed Jerry suspiciously, with not a smile among them. He gathered up his supplies and piled them on the counter. The sound of laughter made him look up; it didn't fit. Three men brushed close by and Jerry knew instantly the source of the foul smell. Their clothes and conduct stamped them as outsiders passing through, not locals. They kept their conversation and laughter between themselves and did not include the Mexican clerk, no sign of familiarity at all. And it wasn't happy laughter born of humor or amusement, but something different. Whatever its reason it pricked the hair on the back of Jerry's neck. When he looked their way they averted their eyes. Jerry pointed to a barrel of bran and nodded to the clerk, who walked over and began scooping some into a gunny sack. When the clerk had sacked enough Jerry nodded again. He paid for his supplies and exited without ever having said a word.

Jerry rode Fan out of town at a brisk trot, unable to shake his uneasy feeling. They passed five or six interconnected pens, some filled with rangy looking longhorns, others with sheep. The vaqueros working in and around the pens stopped what they were doing and stared as he passed. As soon as they were past the pens Jerry slowed Fan to a walk. He thought about hospitable Ernie and the friendly cowboys in the Clovis cafe. *So much for visiting with the locals.*

# 14

## Everything I Learned Comes Down to This

*The Socorro Chieftain*, May 30, 1946 // Magdalena Horse Beats Out Texas
Entry in 2-Day Event // First Geophysics Course in Nation Added by
Socorro's New Mexico School of Mines // Plans for Tuberculosis Hospital
Expansion Okayed

Whoever said that New Mexico skies were enchanted was
right. *No wonder,* Jerry thought, *at this altitude they were
halfway to heaven*: the darkest blue imaginable, awash with
millions of stars and presided over by a sliver of a yellow
moon. The skies were beyond description, the heavenly equivalent of the Texas panhandle and the Llano Estacado rolled
into one.

Jerry made camp a half mile off the highway, not far from
the base of a hill scattered with granite boulders big enough to
be called mountains themselves. A stream that ran along the
base of the hill delivered its melted snow westward, a sure
sign they had crossed the Divide. It was cold but clear, unlike
"Continental Divide Night," the previous night's blizzard that
Jerry swore to remember by that name forever.

After supper Jerry looked over his map and notes. On his
calendar he marked off the previous few days as he drank his
coffee: it was May 30, fourteen days since they had ridden into
Clovis on the heels of a storm. Two weeks of hard riding to
cross the entire state of New Mexico, and two and a half of
those days Fan had spent down with distemper. Already a
dozen miles west of Quemado, tomorrow they would reach Arizona.

Jerry sipped his coffee, reflecting on the trip. Frank and
Rolla had camped on trails like this and no doubt had mar-

76

veled at these same stars. But when they were here they had been dogging a couple thousand head of "the dumbest animals God ever created" (one of Frank's many sayings).

"This is different than any trail drive Frank and Grandpa were ever on," Jerry said in Fan's direction. "With a herd, a remuda, a cook and a chuck wagon, plus a crew of cowboys, they had no reason to be lonesome." The fire burned low. Jerry added some wood and glanced at Fan. "Grandpa and Frank had lots of people to depend on if something went wrong and someone besides their horse to talk to." He looked Fan's way; she hadn't missed a bite. "Are you listening?" Still no response. "I give up on you."

A coyote howled. These mountains were coyote country; Jerry had spotted packs of them during the day. Every night one would begin to howl, like now, then quickly be joined by a host of others, all together sounding like tormented cries from hell. By comparison the hoot owl's call from a nearby tree sounded sweet. In between their howls, Jerry heard sounds he'd grown to know.

Wind whistled through the tall pines. The campfire snapped and popped, adding its rhythm to Mother Nature's primitive song – reassuring, familiar sounds that signaled the end of another day on the trail. Jerry appreciated the fire. After night settled it was a cowboy's savior, comfort, and succor for a solitary soul. He looked up in surprise. Fan had moved closer, with sprigs of grass sticking out at all angles from her mouth. "What's the matter? I thought you'd be munching away half the night out there. Coyotes making you nervous?" Fan went right to the spot where Jerry had dumped her rolled oats. She delicately scoured the dirt with her muzzle, picking up every last morsel.

He chuckled. "I shouldn't complain about how much you eat. You're what got me this far."

Jerry stretched out on top of his bedroll, his head propped against Fan's saddle. "We've just about done it, girl, crossed these mountains that worried me so much." He closed his eyes, not yet ready to sleep, savoring new feelings – anticipation and accomplishment, a dose of confidence.

Suddenly Jerry sat straight up on his bedroll. A sixth sense pricked the hair on the back of his neck. *Movement. Something or someone.* He rose, and with the efficient movements of a seasoned cowboy, made a few adjustments to his camp. Jerry grabbed his Winchester .22, took a quick look around camp, and then disappeared silently into the darkness. Away from the campfire his all-black clothes helped him blend into the night.

He listened carefully. *Three sets of footsteps.* The footfalls told Jerry that three men had fanned out in a circle and were sneaking up on his camp from the northwest. A cold, biting wind of ten, maybe fifteen miles an hour whipped steadily from the same direction as the sound of branches breaking and boots landing softly on rock-strewn ground.

He tucked his six-foot frame behind an outcropping of granite boulders that separated his camp from a nearby creek. The boulders' gritty solid surface, icy against his shoulder, would be a powerful shield against bullets. Jerry peered around toward the creek in back of him and then scanned in every direction, his blue eyes searching the night for a moving shape. Nothing.

Jerry's hiding spot offered a good view of the campfire. Fanned by a strong breeze the sap-filled wood burst into flame, bright hot and hissing, sending blue-tipped, orange tendrils into the air. Away from the heat the intense cold stung his high cheekbones and square jaw, clean-shaven and still warm from the fire. Without his hat his dark collar-length hair offered little protection against the biting cold. Jerry's Stetson was in camp, lying askew on his bedroll as though in his panic he had thrown it down and fled. His coffee mug and supper plate lay upside down in the dirt. The skillet and his utensils had been tossed haphazardly near the fire to reinforce that impression. It was important to make whoever was out there think they had frightened him off.

At the first noise Fan had stopped grazing and raised her head, ears forward in a study of alertness and fear. Jerry could hear her pawing and whinnying, struggling against her restraint. There hadn't been time to check the picket rope. Praying that it would hold, he forced himself to breathe evenly, remembering the warnings and lessons his grandfather and Frank had drummed into him: *You gotta have eyes in the back of your head. Trust your instincts. Pay attention to footsteps. They'll tell you how many, the direction, and how fast they're comin'. Always keep your head. Be as cool as the gun you're holdin'.*

He looked heavenward and said a silent prayer for his training at the hands of two of Oklahoma's most experienced cowboys. His trail skills had been honed razor sharp by his grandfather, his fast-draw, quick as lightening, sharpened by Frank Eaton. No better teacher existed, a man so good and so fast with a gun he'd earned the nickname Pistol Pete and, at seventeen, had been sworn in as a deputy marshal by Isaac Parker, the hanging judge.

*Be cool, you're okay*, he told himself. Jerry's eyes searched the darkness; the footsteps were close now.

Three shadowy figures emerged from the trees. They leapt into the firelight, sweeping their pistols and rifles from side to side in front of them. Their astonished expressions and abrupt movements told Jerry they had expected to surprise their victim. Jerry squinted: *the guys from the store!*

They were a desperate-looking lot. One young man about his own age looked to be short and stocky and had a holster strapped low on his hips, the pistol drawn. The second man had a scruffy beard, wore no hat, and carried a rifle. He looked wild and mean. The third man appeared older, with a slack belly that threatened to explode the buttons from his shirt. His glance darting around camp, the older man moved his rifle back and forth in a half-circle and peered into the darkness in Jerry's direction. Despite the cold, sweat glistened on the fat thief's grimy forehead below the tattered sombrero pushed back on his head. Jerry pulled back and held his breath.

He heard muffled voices speaking rapid Spanish. Exhaling slowly Jerry leaned forward. The youngest thief flipped Jerry's dinner plate upright with the toe of his boot and said something. The older man laughed and set his rifle down against a pine tree. He lifted the edge of his vest to wipe his brow. Jerry spotted a knife handle protruding from a leather holder attached to the belt under the older one's fat stomach. Six inches long, the knife's sheath told Jerry they meant business.

The young stocky thief's posture relaxed; he returned the six shooter to his holster. Their mean-looking companion tossed his Winchester down on the bedroll, its barrel landing with a smack against Fan's saddle. He picked up Jerry's Stetson and placed it on his head. "Que bueno." That much Spanish Jerry understood. The thought of some no-good thief wearing his hat that he'd paid a week's wages for made Jerry grit his teeth; he fought the urge to rush them. "Hang on," he mouthed silently. Jerry tried to slow his breathing; his heart thumped like a war drum. Every muscle in his body felt taut, ready to spring. Frank's Colt .45, all six chambers filled, sat cradled loosely in his tie-down holster. Jerry's forefinger sought the notch carved in the handle.

Frank had carved that notch at age seventeen after he killed Shannon Campsey, one-sixth of the Campsey-Ferber gang that had murdered his father when Frank was seven years old. Five more notches carved farther down stood for the rest of the killers. Their last vision had been of Frank's smoking Colt.

Jerry held his Winchester cocked and ready in his left hand. The thieves conversed again and then laughed – a sinister laughter that spoke volumes that their unintelligible

80

words could not. A shiver crept up Jerry's spine as he heard Fan's whinny. When the man with the sombrero moved toward the pinto Jerry's resolve to be cool evaporated like his breath in the frosty air.

He covered the ten feet to the edge of the camp in a low crouch and lunged into the firelight. The three thieves froze. Jerry's right hand rested lightly on the Colt still in his holster. With his left hand he aimed the rifle squarely at the fat man's sweating forehead.

"Don't touch my horse," he said in a low threatening voice. Jerry's right hand lifted imperceptibly off the Colt, his fingers moving slightly. "You. Toss my hat back on the bedroll, nice and slow. Now."

The desperado reached up and removed the Stetson. As he dropped it, the stocky thief used the diversion to go for his holstered pistol. The fat man made a move for his knife. Lightning fast, Jerry drew his Colt and fired.

"Fill your hand, you sonofabitch." Jerry's words came out automatically; the fury and fierceness in his voice surprised him. The pistol flew out of the young thief's hand, fragments of it exploding in every direction. He screamed, dropped to his knees and grabbed his bloodied hand. Jerry's second shot ripped the fat man's frayed sombrero from his head. His eyes wide with terror, the man sucked in his breath, fingers frozen on the handle of his knife. Jerry nodded at the sheathed weapon. With slow, deliberate movements the fat man removed his fingers from the knife and raised both hands above his head. Almost as a reflex, his eyes darted down at his rifle still leaning against the tree. Jerry fired. The rifle split in half, the bullet rendering a gash in the pine tree where it had stood. Another shot disintegrated the rifle, sending pieces of it flying through the air.

The man on his knees stopped rocking, his cries suspended in midair. "Get up!" Jerry shouted. The injured man struggled to his feet, wiped his face with the sleeve of his good arm, and stared at the Colt Jerry was pointing in his direction. All three men stood silent, waiting. Their expressions said they had intended to kill him, and now that the tables were turned, they fully expected to die.

"Everything I learned comes down to this," Jerry said, glaring at them.

The fat man spoke with a thick accent, exhaling as he did. "Please, señor, don't kill us."

"So you sorry bastards speak English after all." Jerry didn't move. "Make no mistake. If I had wanted to kill you, you'd already be dead."

"Si, we made a big mistake. Please – "

"You're damned right you did. I hear like a wolf and I see like a hawk. And the only man faster than me with a gun is in Oklahoma. You'd better get your friend some help." Jerry nodded at the injured man. "And don't think of coming back. It would be your last mistake. Understand?" The thief hesitated. Jerry fired his fifth shot into the ground at the man's feet.

The fat man turned on his heel and took off in the dark, the other two right behind him. Jerry heard them crashing through the thick brush, grunting and shouting, panic fueling their flight – boots pounding hard earth in terrified retreat.

Jerry went to Fan and stood with his hand on her withers, his ear cocked in the direction of the diminishing sounds. Far in the distance he heard a car motor grind, crank to life, and roar off, then it, too, was gone. Finally it was quiet, a quiet so intense that Jerry could hear his heart thudding in his chest, hear his own breathing, uneven and fast. He didn't know whether to laugh, to shake with fear, or shout at the top of his lungs.

Refilling the chambers of his Colt, Jerry made his way through the brush and trees, following after the thieves until he could see the highway. Nothing there but darkness and silence. Not even the coyotes dared make a sound. He holstered his gun and returned to camp.

Jerry stood at the edge of darkness, his heart refusing to slow. On fire with a feeling he could not name, he stared hard at the sky. From deep inside, instinctive and irrepressible, came emotion clawing and fighting its way to the surface. Around and through restraint and vigilance, it struggled for expression. Jerry threw back his head and howled at the stars. He howled long and high like the wolf. Closing his eyes, he did it again. And again.

Jerry howled a triumphant, victorious, long-wailing cry over mountains that reached halfway to heaven, over endless country, fear, and loneliness, over men who used darkness – men who would kill for a horse and a hat.

Fan whinnied; he could hear her struggling. Jerry stopped. She was as frightened of him as she had been of the three men. He drew a deep breath and went to Fan, stroked her forehead, rubbed down between her frightened eyes, rubbed her soft muzzle.

"It's okay, girl, it's okay," he said softly. "There's nothing to be afraid of. Nothing ever again."

# 15

## Sleepin' on the Job

*The Socorro Chieftain*, May 31, 1946 // Materials Shortage Holds Up Construction of 21 New State Post Office Buildings // Socorro Police Chief Baca & Son Injured in Auto Accident // Hwy 60 Construction Leaves 35 Unpaved Miles to Arizona Border

Jerry found it impossible to fall asleep after the desperados fled. He jumped at every sound and dozed off once, only to awaken suddenly and find himself sitting up with his gun drawn. Using the fire's light he packed up his camp, and as soon as daylight appeared, he and Fan got underway. The adrenaline released by the run-in with the thieves, coupled with the lack of sleep, took its toll. With the late afternoon sun warm on his chest, Jerry fought to keep his eyes open but lost the battle. He released the reins, and they went slack. On her own Fan slowed to a rhythmic, rocking walk. Jerry's head drooped, chin on his chest; finally he fell sound asleep in the saddle.

Later, when Fan tired and came to a halt, Jerry woke up. The sun had already set; it was getting dark fast. "What the hell? Where are we?" He dismounted quickly and looked around. Fan immediately began searching for something to eat.

They were in a flat-bottomed draw about thirty feet wide with boulders on both sides; sparse dry grass grew along the outer edges. A few red cedars, dead long ago, stood with their bleached branches pointing in every direction like ghostly stick figures. Jerry picketed Fan on a fifteen-foot length of rope to a thick tree trunk near the rocks. "You must be starving. And thirsty. You're used to being fed and watered three times a day."

Fully awake now, Jerry scrambled, knowing he had no more than twenty minutes of light, not enough to find them a better camp. He poured out a full measure of grain for Fan and hurriedly gathered up slash from around the base of the trees. With the addition of dead branches and some tenacious prodding the fire finally started. Dark had settled in by the time Fan finished off her pile of grain and came looking for water. Jerry poured all but a few cups of water from his canteen into the bucket and she emptied it quickly. "I'm sorry, girl. That's all there is. We'll have to find water first thing in the morning."

Jerry used the rest of the water to make coffee; he desperately needed something hot to drink. He couldn't see to hunt and he shuddered at the thought of beans for supper. Instead he opened a can of peaches and ate them, anything to stop his rumbling stomach. The fire burned down quickly; it needed leaves, pine cones, anything flammable in order to survive until morning. Searching as far as the fire's waning light would reach, he gathered all the wood he could find and fed the fire until it blazed hot again. He checked to make sure Fan was tethered securely, then spread his bedroll between the fire and the rocks and climbed in. Despite having slept in the saddle he fell asleep immediately.

When the ground began to rumble Jerry did not awaken, instead incorporating the unfamiliar noise into his dream. But when the earth beneath him started shaking and the rumbling grew louder, he awoke with a start. Disoriented and heart pounding, Jerry grabbed his hat, scrambled out of his bedroll, and jammed his feet in his boots. "Fan!" he screamed, his voice lost in the great roar that enveloped them.

A solid black mass – stampeding mustangs with heads tossed high and tails flying – raced by, flank to flank. Inches away hooves pounded, their noise exploding like thunder in

85

his ears. "Heeyyahh!" Jerry hollered. "Heeyyahh!" he screamed as the mustangs surged closer and slammed him against the rocks. The heat of their bodies and their panicked breathing and excited whinnies flowed so close that Jerry felt a part of it. Their sheer power threatened to pull him in.

The herd thundered through the fire, throwing sparks up into the air, creating a choking, blinding cloud of ashes that engulfed the draw. The mustangs called to Fan and she called back. "Heeyyahh!" Jerry waved his hat and shouted as loud as he could. He swung his arms and kept hollering until the smoke and dust overwhelmed him and he could holler no more. Then, just as suddenly as they had come, they were gone.

The sound of their retreating hooves diminished quickly, leaving only the choking haze as evidence of their brief, violent appearance. Dazed and coughing, Jerry stood on trembling legs, frozen to the spot, and stared into the darkness after them. Fan's whinnies and the sound of her rearing and kicking told him she hadn't gotten away. He stumbled toward her, staying well away from her flying hooves. Jerry used the sharp command he'd practiced with her in Oklahoma to quiet her. "Quit. Fan, quit." She whinnied loudly, still prancing and rearing.

He grabbed the end of her picket rope from the tree and held tightly, trying the reprimand again in a softer, calmer voice. "Easy, Fan, it's me. Come on, settle down girl." He slowly reeled in her rope, talking softly and inching closer. She whinnied and snorted and tossed her head. He applied a downward pressure on the rope and murmured softly to her, stroking her neck until she, too, calmed down. "Easy, girl, you don't want to go with them." Jerry ran his hand down her shoulder and front leg; it was trembling as bad as his own. "Like hell you don't." He kept his hand on Fan's flank and when he felt her relax he relaxed.

Jerry pulled a wooden match from his pocket and struck it on a nearby rock. He located his bedroll then straightened it out and climbed back in. He could do nothing else until daylight. Except for the few glowing embers the horses had scattered across the draw, the night was pitch black. The air began to clear and Jerry's heartbeat finally slowed. He had no idea where they were or what had happened to his Stetson.

When he opened one eye the next morning, the sun and Fan were already up. Fan stood over him, nudging his shoulder and nickering for him to get up. Jerry opened his other eye. "Some welcoming party your friends gave us last night." He got up and pulled on his boots. Not a trace of last night's fire remained, no black earth where it had been, no charred bits of wood, no evidence there had ever been a fire at all.

Jerry spotted a hollowed-out path in the middle of the draw where the earth had been pulverized to a fine powder by thousands of pounding hooves. Why had they picked this particular path? Jerry followed it down and around a bend; fifty yards ahead he found the answer. At the bottom of the well-traveled path, the land leveled out and led directly into a small lake.

"Well, if that doesn't beat all." He walked back up to Fan. She was waiting for him with her ears perked forward, straining against her rope. "You stopped right in the middle of a major mustang highway, missy."

Something caught Jerry's eye. Smashed in the dirt up against the rocks lay the remnants of his beautiful black Stetson, the one he had paid thirty-five hard-earned dollars for when he got out of the navy. What remained no longer even resembled a hat. It was stomped and shredded and now it contained more dirt than fabric. "This thing wouldn't do to put on a scarecrow. Your friends did a fine job."

Jerry looked down at his clothes. He looked almost as bad. "Okay, I know where you can drink your fill and we can wash off this dirt. And I'm telling you right now, lady, that's the last time I go to sleep in the saddle and let *you* pick our campsite."

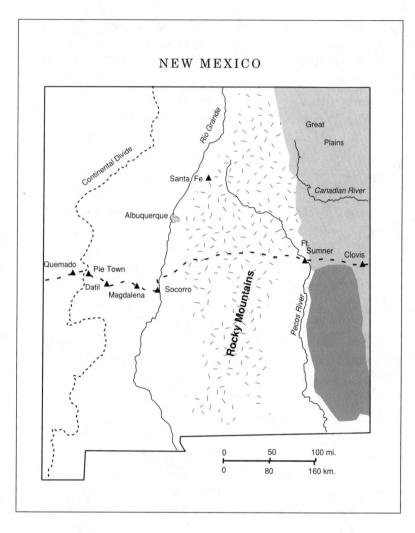

NEW MEXICO

Continental Divide

Rio Grande

Great
Plains

Canadian River

Santa Fe ▲

Albuquerque

Ft.
Sumner    Clovis

Quemado    Pie Town

Datil

Magdalena    Socorro

Rocky Mountains

Pecos River

| 0 | 50 | 100 mi. |
| 0 | 80 | 160 km. |

# 16

## Civilization

*Apache County Independent News*, June 1, 1946 // Truman Creates Central Intelligence Agency // Springerville Man Wins Magdalena Calf-Roping Event // Care Packages Provide Basics to War-Ravaged Europeans

Jerry discovered that Fan had done well on her impromptu navigation. She had maintained a westerly heading, finally coming to a stop a mile off the highway that led to Springerville, Arizona. They backtracked to the highway and headed due west. Fifteen miles later they reached the outskirts of their first Arizona town.

After all that had happened, Jerry felt like kissing the ground when he saw signs of civilization. He spotted the water tower first. Several church spires rose from the town's small skyline, and visible rows of evenly spaced round treetops told him that people had planted shade trees. Jerry spotted something else, though he rubbed his eyes in disbelief at what he saw. Up ahead sat a huge statue beside the road, something that looked like it belonged in a museum. Jerry rode up and dismounted.

Atop a base as tall as he stood the statue of a young woman in a flowing dress and wearing a bonnet on her head, with a baby in her arms and a youngster clinging to her skirts. In weathered bronze, her face glowed in soft patina, beautiful and strong and gentle at the same time. She looked no older than he. She had no doubt been through everything he had been through and more, and she had cared for two children in the process. Jerry squinted to read the inscription: "Madonna of the Trail. A Tribute to pioneers of Arizona and the Southwest who trod this ground and braved the dangers of the Apache and other warrior tribes."

Jerry had wished for a dose of civilization after his encounter with the thieves. The statue, humbling in its message, came as a clear sign that the town up ahead was exactly that. Bathed in sunshine with its skyline of church spires, roofs, and trees, and set against a backdrop of mountains thick with Ponderosa pines, no town had ever looked as good. Elms and sycamores and neat clapboard houses lined the side streets. And the first men Jerry spotted were regular-looking, clean-shaven, jeans and John B—wearing cowboys, men who touched the brims of their Stetsons in recognition of a fellow cowhand riding past.

Highway 60 served as Main Street, and the town was definitely civilized. The marquee of El Rio Theatre caught Jerry's eye. "Now Playing: Jimmy Wakely in *Moon Over Montana*." And coming on Saturday, *The Postman Always Rings Twice* with Lana Turner and John Garfield. People strolled the sidewalks, pausing to visit with one another. Cars and horses hooked to wagons occupied curb space in front of some of the stores. A water tower with "Springerville" painted on its side loomed above everything at the far end of town. "This place reminds me of home, Fan. I like this town."

Jerry stopped first at Becker Mercantile Company on Main Street. They had Denim Riders for two dollars and ninety-eight cents a pair. He considered buying two pair but he already had one extra and Fan didn't need to carry more weight than necessary. He did buy a new black Stetson. The day's ride in the sun without a hat had caused his face to feel hot and tender. Next door at Western Drug Company a white-coated pharmacist with glasses perched on the end of his nose sold Jerry the Unguentine ointment he needed. A soda fountain covered the length of the side wall. In back of the counter were giant pictures of milk shakes and cones and banana splits that looked good enough to make his mouth water. A slight-built boy wearing what looked like a paper chef's hat atop his unruly hair was busy waiting on customers.

Jerry spied the flavor he wanted. "Everything looks delicious. How about a cone with a big scoop of strawberry."

"Yessir, strawberry it is." The boy grabbed a spoon and dipped it in water then jammed a scoop of ice cream flecked with strawberries down into a cone. On top of that he piled a mound of ice cream so huge it hung over the sides. "That'll be five cents, sir. Is that big enough for you?"

Jerry handed him a nickel though he could only nod and smile, hurriedly licking around the edge to keep it from dripping. He walked outside and sat down on a bench, completely absorbed in eating. Closing his eyes, he was transported back home to the Guthrie kitchen; he was ten years old again and he and his brothers were eating their father's special homemade ice cream. He opened his eyes to see Fan staring at him. Suddenly overcome with guilt, Jerry jumped up. "How could I forget you? I know what you like as much as I like ice cream."

Jerry went back into Becker's and while he finished his cone he bought supplies and a half-dozen apples. When he came out of the store Fan met him halfway across the sidewalk before he could get to her. She jammed her nose into the bag of apples, expecting *something*.

"I know how you feel. Let me cut one up." Jerry popped the last of the cone in his mouth and cut a wedge out of an apple with his pocket knife. Fan's muzzle moved lightly across his palm, and the apple wedge disappeared. He cut up two apples and put the rest into his saddlebags.

"Another one tomorrow, okay? You deserve some kind of reward for not running off with those mustangs." She smacked and slurped, as happy over her treat as Jerry had been with his. Jerry wrote a letter to Rolla and Frank while Fan ate. He planned to write to his mother and father when he reached Phoenix.

Across the street a barber pole spiraled slowly in its glass cylinder on the front of Troy's Barbershop. Jerry had promised himself to get a haircut ever since Socorro Police Chief Baca had questioned him because of his shaggy appearance. Jerry followed daily grooming habits that were formed by his mother and father long ago and that were constantly emphasized by Rolla Goodnight. Pride in one's appearance was ingrained in him as surely as his cowboy skills.

In truth, as much as he wanted a haircut, Jerry wanted to spend time – however short – in the company of men like himself; he wanted to connect again with a familiar world. He led Fan across the street and tied her to a post in front of the shop. Lorene's Beauty Shop sat next to Troy's; a pretty blond girl inside the shop smiled at him through the window. Jerry smiled and touched the brim of his hat. *Must not look as bad as I thought.*

Jerry opened the barbershop door and took a deep breath. The sharp scent of clean, fragrant shaving soaps and aftershave greeted him. *Lord that smells good. Why have I never really noticed that before?* The polished black and white squares on the floor glistened in the afternoon sun. Two chairs, one of them occupied, filled the small shop. The barber standing behind the empty chair shook out a white drape with a crisp snap. "Name's Troy. Have a seat." Jerry hung his new hat on the rack and closed the door.

"Nice-looking John B. Get that at Becker's?" Troy fastened the drape around Jerry's neck, ran a comb through his hair, and started snipping.

"Sure did. Now I need a haircut. I look too shaggy to be wearing such a good-looking Stetson."

"It does look like it's been a while since you had a cut."

"Eight hundred and fifty miles ago."

"Where's your rig? I see your horse out there."

"She *is* my rig."

The barber's hands paused in midair. "You rode eight hundred and fifty miles on her?" They both looked out at Fan; she was asleep, with one rear hoof resting on its edge and her eyes half-closed. "How long did that take?" Troy resumed cutting Jerry's hair.

"What's the date today?"

"The first of June."

"Well, then, it took us twenty-nine days."

Troy chuckled. "Amazing. No wonder she's napping. Either the law's after you or you got woman trouble."

The other barber nudged his customer. The patron, his face covered by a hot towel, lifted the corner and peeked out at Jerry.

Jerry smiled. "Nah, just making a trip for my grandfather."

"Where you headed on this trip, if you don't mind my asking?"

"Hollywood."

"California?" Troy let out a low whistle. "Virgil. Oliver. Did you hear that? This fella's on his way to Hollywood."

Virgil looked up from the steady slip-slap of his straight-edge razor against a leather strap. "You mean *the* Hollywood, the one where they make movies?"

Jerry smiled. "That's the one."

"You picked a danged slow way to get there," Troy said.

"Not too slow, I hope. I've got to get there in fifty days to win the bet."

With that, the man under the hot towel sat up and removed it from his face. "Now that sounds like a story. Hold up, Virgil, I want to hear this." His face glowed pink from the heat and his voice had an admiring tone.

Troy stopped cutting. "Oliver's right, you can't say something like that then leave us hanging."

The three men looked at Jerry expectantly.

"Okay, but you've got to keep cutting. The clock's ticking on that bet and I need to get going." Troy's scissors began snipping again in a fast rhythm. "You ever heard of Charles Goodnight?" Jerry asked.

Troy let out a low whistle. "You bet. The Hashknife Ranch was near here in the old days, the biggest spread in the territory. Story was, half of Charlie Goodnight's hands ended up wrangling for the Hashknife because he ran them off for drinking or gambling. Hashknife boys were a rowdy bunch."

Virgil spoke up. "But Charlie Goodnight's been dead damned near twenty years. What's he – "

"What about Frank "Pistol Pete" Eaton. Ever hear of him?" Jerry asked.

"Can't say that I have," Virgil said. The others shook their heads.

"Frank's pretty famous in Oklahoma, Kansas, and Texas. So famous, in fact, they copied his mustache and ten gallon hat and made his likeness the mascot of Oklahoma State University. That's Pistol Pete."

"I'd say that qualifies as being famous," Troy said.

"Frank used to be a gunfighter when he was young, one of Isaac Parker's deputy marshals. He's my granddad's best friend and like another grandfather to me. Frank's the one who gave me this six-shooter and the mare so I could make the ride."

"Is he the one who made the bet?" Oliver said.

"No, my granddad did. With Jimmy Wakely."

"Hold on a minute," Virgil said. "Are you talking about Jimmy Wakely the movie star?" Virgil was clearly impressed.

"The very one that's in the movie at the El Rio Theater," Jerry said. "That's the first thing I saw when I rode into town."

"This just keeps gettin' better. Gunfighters and movie stars, what's next?" Oliver threw aside his drape and leaned forward in his chair.

The more Jerry talked the faster Troy's scissors flew. Jerry hoped he knew what he was doing.

"When Jimmy Wakely came to Oklahoma last September to take part in the Cherokee Strip celebration, he told my grandfather that real cowboys are finished. That they're soon

94

gonna be a thing of the past. And then he said there isn't a cowboy around worth his salt anymore who could sit in a saddle for the length of a trail drive. That didn't sit well with Grandpa – at all. That's when he bet Jimmy I could ride from Oklahoma to Hollywood in fifty days or less. It's about fifteen hundred miles, same as a trail drive."

"Fifteen hundred miles in fifty days. Your grandfather must have a lot of faith in you," Troy said. Virgil and Oliver agreed. "I'm being nosey but I have to ask, how much was this bet?" Troy asked.

"Grandpa never would say how much he bet. I don't know."

"I still don't see what Charlie Goodnight has to do with this," Oliver said.

"Charlie and my grandfather were cousins. Charlie taught him the cattle business and turned him into a cowboy. Then Grandpa taught me. Well, him and Frank Eaton. My grandfather is Rolla Goodnight, owns the Bar R Ranch out of Enid, Oklahoma." Jerry felt a surge of pride.

Troy looked puzzled. "Okay, your grandfather wins a bet and collects some unknown amount of money from a movie star, but what do you get? Why are you risking your neck?"

The question instantly brought to mind the image of the three desperados. "Good question. I guess I wanted to prove Jimmy wrong, wanted to live up to the Goodnight tradition my grandfather believes in so much. When it comes right down to it, though, I really wanted to prove to myself I could do it."

Troy removed Jerry's drape and shook it gently, covering the floor beneath his chair with clumps of dark hair. "This haircut is on the house. I cut practically every cowboy's hair around Springerville, and I'd lay odds that not one of them would ride fifteen hundred miles to prove a point or win a bet if he didn't get the money. I hope you'll let us know when you make it." Troy scribbled his name and address on a piece of paper and handed it to Jerry.

"That's mighty nice of you. I will drop you a card. It was a pleasure getting to meet the three of you." Jerry placed the paper in his wallet and put on his new Stetson. Troy, Virgil, and Oliver each shook his hand and then followed him out of the shop, slapping him on the back and laughing. Across the street three cowboys exited Becker's.

Troy hollered at them. "Come on over here. You gotta meet this fella."

Jerry stood by and listened as his three admirers did the talking. They spilled out his story, interrupting each other, punctuating it with nods and raised eyebrows and a reverent tone when one said "Hollywood" and another said "mooovie star." The cowboys listened attentively and shot Jerry quick, approving glances when someone mentioned the Goodnight name. Jerry rode away to a chorus of good-byes and shouts of good luck. He mailed his letter to Rolla and Frank just before the post office closed up for the evening.

"Okay, Fan, we still have a good two or three hours of riding time left."

# 17

## Geronimo Country

*Apache County Independent News,* June 1, 1946 // Robson Wins Indy 500 with Record 114.8 MPH // Round Valley Mormons Play Host to Top Church Officials // Memorial Day Services Include Tribute to Brothers Gilbert, Malcolm, Jerold Greer

Jerry looked back over his shoulder at the neon El Rio Theatre sign flashing pink, green, and white. "Places like that offset the bad times, don't you think, Fan?" Fan's ears flicked back and forth but otherwise she gave no response. "It would be nice if you could talk. This trip would be a lot more interesting." The thought of Fan talking made Jerry smile. After some of their adventures it was very likely he might not want to hear what she had to say at all.

"I've proved something. So have you, girl, even if it's to nobody but you and me." Jerry's smile deepened. The image of the discharged, crippled-up seaman-student full of doubts about himself had vanished along with his fears about his back. The anguish and fear so real only a few months ago now seemed like a long-ago bad dream.

Everywhere he looked Jerry saw lush pastures filled with fat Herefords; others held sheep. Troy had mentioned that John Wayne owned a ranch around Springerville, a tantalizing thought that maybe they were riding over his property. It stirred images of gunslingers and range wars between cattlemen and sheepmen.

"You're riding over famous ground, Fan. Some of the biggest gunfighters in the territory used to hang out here. The Clanton gang, all one hundred of them, lived around here. Byron knows all about Ike and the two other Clantons shooting it out with Wyatt Earp and Doc Holiday at the OK Corral. And Butch Cassidy and Billy the Kid did their carousing in town, at different times, of course. Byron would love it here. I'd never get him to leave." Fan gave no acknowledgment. Jerry applied a little pressure with his knees and Fan snorted. "That's better."

Jerry dropped south of the highway and rode alongside the White River through alpine-like meadows blanketed with wild yellow daisies. He passed waterfalls that spilled into the river over volcanic rock thick with brush and outlined in ferns.

He fished for his supper; a big cutthroat practically jumped into his skillet. "Look at this!" Jerry held up the fish in Fan's direction. "Don't you know if Rolla and Frank knew they could put a pole in the water and catch a twelve-inch trout in five minutes they wouldn't want to leave this place either?" Fan, busy grazing on the thick grass, did not look his way. Jerry whistled and she raised her head, ears alertly forward. Fan walked over to him. "Atta girl. You never know when we might get separated. I need to be able to count on you." Jerry rewarded her with an apple.

Few signs of man existed to interrupt the tranquillity. Jerry spotted white tail deer, free-roaming elk, and pronghorn antelope herds. One morning he caught a glimpse of a distant brown bear with her two cubs. It didn't matter in which direction Jerry gazed; he saw dramatic landscape. Majestic peaks carpeted with pines, firs, and spruce loomed high on both sides. At the base of the mountains stood thick stands of aspens, their white trunks and pale shimmering leaves contrasting sharply against the dark ponderosas and silvery blue-green spruce. It wasn't until he passed the Fort Apache Timber Company the next day that he realized they were on reservation land. The whine of machines filled the stillness, and Jerry breathed in the acrid smell of lumber processing instead of cool pine-scented forest air.

They reached the Mogollon Rim at midday. Jerry took Fan's saddle off and she immediately rolled in the dirt. "You love that. Why is that? You like the way it scratches your skin or do you just like getting dirty?" He watered and fed her and Fan slept while he fixed his own lunch. Jerry ate his meal, all the while looking out over yet another incredible vista.

The Mogollon Rim, the shelf where the Colorado Plateau ended, towered three thousand feet above the southwest desert. He looked out over hills and rocks, cliffs, canyons, and mesas – an earthen maze of red and gold and every shade of brown. Phoenix waited for them somewhere out there in the distance. The desert. Thoughts of *the desert* conjured up visions of searing heat, unquenchable thirst, and endless sand. At a gut level it stirred the same fear as Jerry's first glimpse of the Texas panhandle and the Rockies.

His concern proved to be unfounded. This eastern edge of the Arizona desert, at five thousand feet elevation, was warm not hot, and Jerry found plenty of full creeks. He reminded himself that the land around him had once been home to Geronimo; and, like the history of the Llano Estacado, the thought of the Apache chief made him ride taller in the saddle.

Once they were out of the canyons, Jerry held the reins loosely, and Fan settled into her jog and lope gait. They passed Apache houses – eight-sided mud and log hogans – all with gardens close by. Every home had a large patch of corn planted, lush and green and about ankle high. Some had horses tethered in front, and all hogans had children playing outside. At one a woman sat cross-legged on a mat near the blanket-covered opening. Her hands flew back and forth across a loom, the rhythm of their movement interrupted occasionally to push a wooden cradle. She glanced Jerry's way but quickly looked back at her work.

Jerry rode past buckboards and horse-drawn wagons overflowing with Indian families. He passed groups of Apache men and boys riding bareback. Some dressed like white men.

Others, especially the younger ones, wore only leather vests over their bare chests with long leather pants fringed down the side. All of them had long black hair, either flowing loosely or tied into braids. And none of them gave Jerry more than a curious glance.

At Cibecue, an Apache trading-post village, Jerry got to see where all of them were headed: an all-Indian rodeo had just started when he rode in. Four hours of daylight remained but he couldn't let Fan ride any farther. They had covered thirty-five miles since early morning, half of which had been in the high country. She needed rest.

The Cibecue Trading Post seemed to be headquarters for the rodeo's activities. Horses stood side by side, tethered to the rail in front. Some resembled Fan in color and marking except that none of them wore saddles.

Across the dirt field near the trading post, horse-drawn wagons and buckboards of every description were parked every which way. Jerry found a shady place and picketed Fan to a hitching rail nailed to a tree a short distance away. While he was wondering whether he should let her drink at the watering trough nearby, Fan proceeded to stick her muzzle in and began drinking before he could dismount.

Jerry looked around for other white people but found none. It seemed odd that the Apaches gave him nothing more than a passing glance; he gratefully moved among them unacknowledged. He walked among old men deep in conversation, their bronzed faces etched with lines; they looked ancient and full of wisdom. The old ones spoke words delivered with a cadence and guttural softness that sounded musical but were unintelligible to the young cowboy. Out of the corner of his eye Jerry watched an elder remove his hat to wipe his brow. He wore his gray hair braided in two long braids and coiled into a perfect circle on top of his head. After he had wiped his brow on his sleeve the Apache placed the hat back on top to hold the coil in place. Jerry smiled, silently reminding himself to tease Frank that he'd found him a new hairdo for his braids.

Jerry walked close to short, brown grandmothers with silvery hair and missing teeth, young mothers with babies strapped to their backs, and lean young men strutting like roosters in front of smiling girls. The women wore long velvet skirts decorated with silver beads and conch shells. Calf-length moccasins peeked from under their skirts as they walked and moved. All wore their hair in braids, and except for a few very young girls, all were plump. Some of the children spoke English to their playmates and received an answer back in Apache. They scooted around and by Jerry, laughing and shouting, raising clouds of red dust as they chased each other and their skinny, yapping dogs.

Jerry walked up to a large arena surrounded by onlookers, rested his arms on the fence and watched. Inside the enclosure a bronc rider still attached to his bareback mount whooped and hollered as the wild-eyed sorrel tried to dislodge him.

Nearby, two rows of makeshift tents sold food, filling the air with smoke and some of the best smells Jerry had ever inhaled. Following one pungent sweet aroma to its source, he bought hot Indian fry bread. He ate beef and wild game cooked over open flame and ears of multicolored corn, just plucked from boiling water, that was sweet and finger-burning hot. One woman sold roasted piñon nuts. Another offered hot tortillas made from the corn she had ground on a metate, patted into rounds, and fried over a fire in front of her tent. Women were in charge of selling the food. Jerry held out his palm covered with coins and nodded for them to take what they wanted for the food. Pudgy fingers moved across his palm like Fan's muzzle collecting an apple wedge. They picked out a nickel for the bread or two pennies for an ear of corn. Jerry saw no liquor, but everywhere stacked in the shade he saw wooden crates with bottles of orange, grape, and raspberry soda pop. And it seemed that every man, woman, and child had one of the bottles in their hands.

He stayed until twilight, watching Brahma and longhorn bull-riding, calf-roping, and bronc-riding events. When later he made camp alongside Cibecue Creek south of the trading post Jerry ate more Indian fry bread, more meat, and more ears of corn, until he felt stuffed. After Fan drank her fill and ate a large portion of grain, she polished off the corn cobs Jerry saved for her.

It had been a special day, getting to be among the Apache people in their world; it was a day Jerry wanted to remember: young people flirting, elderly men trading stories, and bright-eyed grandchildren clinging to skirts while their grand-mothers cooked and laughed – sharing something that would be forever unknown to a white man. This was a rare gift, getting to peel aside a curtain and glimpse into a culture as ancient as this land they called home. Again, Jerry silently thanked his grandfather for making the bet.

He lit a match and quickly rechecked his map. The Salt River Canyon lay sixteen miles ahead, directly in their path to Phoenix. Several forks of the White River, the Black River, and farther west, the Canyon, Cibecue, and Carrizo Creeks flowed into the Salt River. It looked to be of a pretty good size, and it ran right through the canyon they had to cross. "Water ahead, Fan. Bath time, laundry time. You love water, you're going to love this."

# 18

## The Letter

*The Guthrie Daily Leader*, June 8, 1946 // World Food Crisis Prompts War Dept Study of Farmers' Early Discharge // Tojo Pleads Innocent Before Int'l Tribunal to Charges of Aggression, Plunder, War

Rolla Goodnight exited Taylor's Trading Company, his arms loaded with groceries. He headed toward his truck parked down Main Street near the blacksmith shop where he'd left Frank. As Rolla passed Marshall's post office the door opened and the postmistress stuck her head out. In an obvious state of excitement she waved at him, a letter in her hand. "Oh, Mr. Goodnight, I'm glad I found you. I have a letter here, just came in. It's from Jerry. From Arizonaah."

"Well, I sure thank you for flaggin' me down. I appreciate it. Could you drop it in my grocery bag?" Rolla walked a few more steps then put the bags down and extracted the letter. Trying to make out the postmark, he held it at arm's length and was squinting at it when he heard a voice behind him.

"Hello, Mr. Goodnight." He turned around to find Carlton Scheir, one of Jerry's high school friends.

"Afternoon, Carlton. What are you up to?"

"On my way to my new job. Mister and Missus Taylor hired me to stock shelves. Have you heard from Jerry?"

"Got his first letter right here. We had one postcard from New Mexico. Said Fan had a go-round with distemper. I'm anxious to hear what he's got to say." Rolla slipped on his reading glasses. "This one's from Springerville, Arizona, so his horse must have come out okay."

"That sure is something, him riding all the way to California. I'd be afraid of doing something like that."

"Is that right, a young fellow like yourself? Why, you can do anything you set your mind to."

Carlton shook his head. "You sound like my dad. But when he says it, he's just talking about me going to Phillips University and majoring in business, not riding a horse halfway across the coun – "

"Cowboys been doing what Jerry's doing since before I was born. Wish I coulda gone with him. I haven't ridden through that part of the country since I helped Charlie Goodnight take some herds through sixty years ago."

"I heard you made some kind of a bet with Jimmy Wakely. If anybody can win it, Jerry can. If he calls, please be sure to tell him everyone round here is rooting for him, especially me."

"I'll make it a point to pass that along to his mama. He'll be calling her."

"Good-bye, sir. Tell Mr. Eaton hello."

The hot sun beat down as Rolla greeted several other Marshall residents. He shuffled grocery bags from one arm to the other each time someone stopped him. One neighbor in bib overalls and his wife in a wash dress stopped to ask about Jerry. Another neighbor came up and tipped his hat then joined in the conversation. Rolla passed three or four more people before he reached his truck. They, too, stopped him and asked about Jerry. Every one of them mentioned how proud he and the family must be of Jerry doing such a fine, brave thing.

Rolla thought about his neighbors' attitudes all the way to his truck, parked in the shade of the Marshall water tower. He put his groceries inside the truck. Most of the neighbors were twenty or thirty years younger than he, and some more than that. They all acted like Jerry's ride was the next hardest thing to fighting on Iwo Jima. Rolla could not understand. A sobering thought, this unexpected attitude, and it made Rolla edgy. It served as a hint that Jimmy might be right. Frank, his holster around his hips, hollered good-bye to the blacksmith and exited his shop. He climbed into the truck.

Top: Jerry on Fan, May 2, 1946. Photo taken for the *Guthrie Daily Leader*. Photo courtesy of Jerry Van Meter and the *Guthrie Daily Leader*.

Bottom: Rolla, Jerry (kneeling), Frank, and Fan on the Chisholm Trail, September, 1945. Photo courtesy of Jerry Van Meter.

Top, left: Jimmy Wakely on Lucky, his movie horse, circa 1945. Photo courtesy of Lindalee Wakely.

Bottom, left: Jerry, age 16, at Guthrie farm with his model planes. Photo courtesy of Jerry Van Meter.

Bottom, right: Rolla and Frank, circa 1946. Photo courtesy of Jerry Van Meter.

Top: Rolla and Frank as young men, 1886. Photo courtesy of Elizabeth Eaton Wise.

Bottom: Charles Goodnight and buffalo head, circa 1888. Photo 1, 568/294. Courtesy of the Panhandle-Plains Historical Museum Research Center, Canyon, Texas.

"Everybody in town knows about the bet, Frank. Is there anybody you missed tellin'?" Rolla said as he started the truck.

"Nosiree, I think I pretty much got everybody. What's got you all riled up? You look like somebody fed you skunk soup."

"Tell me somethin'. How many times did you make a ride like Jerry's?"

"You talkin' me, by myself?"

"Yup." Rolla shifted into first gear and drove the Chevy onto Main Street.

"Half a dozen, prob'ly. With the drives you 'n me did, another dozen."

"I just had ten people tell me what a brave thing Jerry's doing. The postmistress handed me a letter from Jerry and was danged near hopping up and down on one foot about it. I'm thinkin' I think a lot different than these other folks think. What do you think?"

"Soon as I figure out the question I'll answer you." Frank, silent for a moment, waved as they passed a barefooted youngster. "Maybe you need a dose of castor oil." He chuckled quietly.

"You know damn well what I mean."

"Well, nobody thought it was 'specially brave in our day. We did it for a livin'. All cowboys did. I guess it ain't so common anymore, so people are gonna look at it different."

Rolla handed Frank the envelope. "Here's Jerry's letter."

"Want me to read it to you while you drive?" Frank held it up to the sunlight. "You look anxious."

"I ain't worried-anxious. I'm . . . curious-anxious."

"Wait a minute, I need my spectacles." Frank fished wire-rimmed glasses out of his shirt pocket and stretched them behind each ear, one earpiece at a time. He adjusted the envelope to various distances from his eyes.

"How 'bout doing it today? We only got five miles to go."

"Get that hitch outta your getalong now." Frank got out his pocketknife and carefully slit the envelope open.

*Dear Grandpa and Frank.*

"Now ain't that nice, he made it to me, too."

"Well o'course he made it to you, too. Do I have to pull this truck over and take that letter away from you, you ornery old cuss?"

Frank cleared his throat and continued.

*I'm sitting here having an ice cream cone in Springerville, Arizona. It's a nice town after some I've seen. I'm eating pretty good, especially over the Rockies. I had me about every kind of small game there is (thanks, Grandpa). Still, I'm sick of beans. This is the first ice cream I've had and does it taste good. I sure miss Mama's peach cobbler and your biscuits and ham gravy.*

*I'm a little better than half way to Hollywood. This is most surely the hard way, just ask Fan. Ha Ha. She is doing fine now, but thinner I can tell. I've seen some beautiful country. Will be able to tell some trail stories of my own when I get back. Everything you taught me came in handy when I got jumped by three mean-looking Mexicans on the Continental Divide. They meant to kill me and take everything I had. One guy drew on me so I had no choice but to outdraw him (thanks, Frank). The last thing I remember saying before I pulled the trigger was, "fill your hand you SOB." I didn't even realize I said it, it just popped out. I winged the guy and the three of them took off.*

"Well, I'll be dawg!" Frank howled with laughter and slapped his knee.

Rolla hit the steering wheel with the heel of his hand. "Damn them crooks. If that don't beat all. Go ahead, what else does he say?"

*Grandpa, you'll be happy to know that so far a lot of what I've seen doesn't look like it's changed. The Palo Duro looked exactly like you described it. The Llano Estacado west of Clovis must look the same as when you rode through. And Frank, I'm pretty sure Ft. Sumner didn't look much different than when your friend Pat Garrett shot the Kid. Did you get the book? Speaking of Billy, for a day or two I felt like Jerry the Kid. Ha Ha.*

*I'm real glad I made the trip and grateful to be on schedule. Lots of things have happened, but I handled them like you said. I may come out of this a cowboy yet. Thanks to both of you for all you taught me.*

*Your loving grandson and friend, Jerry*

Rolla stared straight ahead, an uneasy feeling gripping him. "I never give it a thought that somebody'd try to kill him. You think he'll be all right?"

Frank was rereading the letter and chuckling. "Fill your hand, you sonofa . . . exactly like I taught him. Quit your worryin', Rolla. Nothin's gonna get the best of Jerry Van Meter. That man's gonna be fine."

# 19

## A River Ran over Us

*Fort Apache Reservation News*, June 4, 1946 // Antelope Herd Increase Noted // Wild Dog Control Ordered by Tribal Council // Fort Apache 4-H Club Hosts 275 Navajo Members

The sixteen miles to the Salt River Canyon turned out to be hard miles. They continually rode up one hill and down another, then up yet another, all the while descending in elevation. Jerry and Fan wound their way through sun-heated arroyos and canyons; Jerry used his compass to navigate through the maze-like landscape. He wanted to get across the river, have lunch, and rest Fan on the other side.

They reached the canyon rim and Jerry began looking for a trail down to the river. Mesquite, sage, and brittlebush thrived in the rock-strewn earth and made finding the canyon's entrance difficult. When he did find it, the path was narrow, steep, rocky, and well worn. The trail hugged the side of the steep canyon for thirty feet down, ending on a flattened-out ridge. The elongated ledge obscured any view of the bottom of the canyon and the river. But, if his map was correct the trail picked up again somewhere along the ridge, for it clearly showed that the trail led all the way to the canyon floor.

They had descended ten feet down when Fan's leg brushed against a mesquite bush on the mountain side of the trail. By the time Jerry saw the rattler coiled in the shade it had already struck at Fan. She shied; her hooves slipped on the decomposed rock, and both of them went over the edge. Jerry had no time to dive off. With his left leg pinned beneath Fan's flank, they slid twenty feet down the steep embankment to the flattened-out ridge below.

When the noise of falling rocks stopped, the only sound interrupting the stillness was their breathing. Fan lay perfectly still as though gauging whether she was hurt. Finally she struggled to her feet. During the fall Jerry had let go of the reins; nothing held her now. "Come on, Fan. Here, girl," Jerry said from the ground. He tried to keep his voice calm, not sure she was okay and worried that if she was she would bolt and run.

Jerry suddenly became aware of his leg, one long bloody scratch that felt like it was on fire. The left leg of his jeans from mid-thigh down to his foot no longer existed; a few small shreds remained, attached only by the inside seam. Struggling to his feet Jerry put his full weight on it. "Thank God it isn't broken," he whispered in relief.

Jerry stepped forward and reached for the reins. Fan backed up. "Come on, girl, don't do this," he said softly. "We're in the middle of nowhere." Fan tossed her head and snorted. He spoke in as soothing a voice as he could muster. "Remember outside Springerville when I said we might get separated and I needed to be able to count on you?" Fan pawed the ground. *She's ready to take off.* Jerry held his outstretched hand steady and whistled an easy whistle. "This is one of those times. Can I count on you, Fan?" He held his breath and waited. Fan seemed to think it over then ambled toward him, nuzzling his outstretched hand. Jerry exhaled a sigh of relief. "You are one great horse, girl. The best."

Jerry gathered her reins and stroked her neck. "Good girl, Fan." He ran his hands down her trembling legs. "No broken bones, no snake bite. Your flank doesn't even have a mark on it." Jerry instantly realized how his leg got so badly scratched: it had held Fan away from the rocky embankment during the slide. He fished an apple out of the saddlebag. "This is for being able to count on you. You earned this."

A sure-footed horse, Fan's fall was bad luck pure and simple. Jerry dismissed it and tried to ignore his stinging leg.

Grateful that they hadn't rolled down the embankment, that his leg hadn't been crushed, and that Fan had come out of the slide uninjured, Jerry said a silent thank you and mounted up. Finding the continuation of the trail he resumed their descent, this time avoiding bushes. The lower part of the trail was four times longer. He kept a close eye on the path and let Fan pick her way. If they went over the edge here it wouldn't matter about the bet or Hollywood or anything else.

Jerry's leg was bleeding, the skin embedded with sand and rocks, throbbing now and stinging even worse. The river would clean away the dirt. As soon as they crossed Jerry intended to put Bag Balm on it. A soothing ointment that no cowboy was ever without, Bag Balm helped cure horses' scrapes and scratches; it would help his raw leg as well.

Jerry heard the river before he saw it. When he rode up to its edge the roar drowned out all other sounds. More than a half mile wide, it almost filled the canyon. The walls on the other side consisted of sage-covered hills that sloped down gently at first, then dropped straight to the water. Higher up, the hills met two tiers of vertical walls that were each five hundred feet high, creating a thousand feet of straight-up canyon wall. Jerry could only stare and try to fight his rising panic. *There's no place to get out of the river even if we do make it across. This couldn't be any more dangerous.*

No ridge or water line showed, indicating that the river was at its highest level. High water and a fast current had ripped out trees on its journey through the canyon, toppling them into the river and gathering debris in their branches.

Directly in front of them and halfway across, the river was split into two raging torrents by an island of massive boulders. The current thundered around and over the boulders, then dropped twenty feet, producing a deafening roar. Kicking up spray a hundred feet into the air it was a breathtaking sight and an impossible place to cross.

Jerry rode for half an hour up and down the narrow bank to find a flat expanse of river where boulders and waterfalls were two less things to worry about. He spotted shallow beaches on the other side and realized their only chance would be to aim for one of those. He dismounted, his heart pounding. Fan waded into the water and started drinking.

"Hang on a minute, will you?" Jerry put his six-shooter in the tin with his calendar and writing pad, tied the saddlebags up on top, and secured the Winchester on top of it all. He hoped it would keep everything out of the water. Jerry looked straight up at the cliff above him. *We can't go back. We'd never make it to Hollywood on time.* He thought about removing his boots and adding them to the pile, but the river bottom looked to be as rocky as the shore. He decided against it.

Jerry patted Fan's neck and shouted, "I know you love water, but I never figured on anything like this. Let's stick together, okay?" He knew she couldn't hear him above the roar, and it didn't matter anyway. This was going to be a roll of the dice. Fan moved into the current and Jerry followed, panic and excitement taking over as icy water poured into his boots. "I hate cold water!" he shouted at the river. Jerry jammed his hat firmly on his head and took hold of Fan's tail. "Okay, Fan, let's swim this damn river."

No sooner had the words left his mouth than the riverbed beneath Jerry's feet disappeared. He felt Fan's body float free and her powerful rear legs displace the water beneath him. Jerry forced himself to breathe evenly and paddle with strong, even strokes with his right hand. He held tight to Fan's tail with his left.

Never had they crossed a river this wide or this wild while training in Oklahoma. Never had they been swept downstream faster than their forward progress. Jerry felt Fan's power pulling them and he paddled and kicked, trying to keep his focus on the far bank. The blur of the canyon walls on the opposite side looked closer; they were making progress. Jerry and Fan reached mid-river. Without warning a strong circular current enveloped them, spinning them round and round, dizzying and disorienting. When they stopped spinning it took a moment for Jerry to get his bearings. They had turned counterclockwise several times; Fan's head pointed down river. The current had slammed him up against her right flank and he could feel her struggling. Fan's front leg brushed dangerously close to his and Jerry pushed away to get out of the way of her powerful hooves. "C'mon, swim for shore!"

He had no idea if Fan heard him. A diagonal wave – a surge of water – swamped Jerry, and he went under. No calm, steady, and even strokes now. He fought to reach the surface, kicking and paddling as hard as he could. Another surge lifted his Stetson and Jerry instinctively let go of Fan's tail and grabbed it. "NO!" he screamed when he realized what he'd done. His voice was lost to the river's roar.

Without Fan's massive weight holding him Jerry floated free, racing down the river and bobbing under and out of the water like a piece of wood. He looked back; Fan's head, a small dot, stuck above the surface of the choppy water, and then he couldn't see her at all. Because of his water-filled boots Jerry raced down the river nearly vertical in the water, fighting with everything he had to keep his head up. When he surfaced he dodged boulders and free-floating logs. Battling the water's force, Jerry watched canyon walls race by at a frightening speed. He took a breath, clamped the brim of his hat between his teeth, and started kicking and pulling through the water. Every muscle burned like fire.

Jerry coughed and choked and swallowed river water through gritted teeth, refusing to give up a second hat on this trip. The canyon curved, its walls closer together now, narrower and higher, compressing the river's flow. Jerry felt the water rise like a bucking bronco, roaring ever higher. With the opposite bank closer, he battled with renewed energy. Ahead, and coming up fast, he saw a dead tree angled into the water – a chance. The icy waters had numbed his arms and legs; Jerry hoped they would cooperate. With a burst of en-

112

ergy he pulled himself in line with the tree. It was coming right at his face. He had a split second to stick his arms out in front and give a kick to raise his head. Jerry hit the tree square on with the upper part of his chest. He wrapped his arms around it, closed his eyes and hung on. How long he remained that way he had no idea, but when he opened his eyes he was ten feet away from the bank. It took a concentrated effort for him to unclench his jaws. When he felt a sharp pain on both sides of his neck, Jerry knew he had succeeded. Jamming the Stetson back on his head, he began pulling toward shore. The river's force smashed him against the tree as he inched his way along. The rough bark and broken branches ripped his shirt and scratched his chest and arms; he felt nothing. Then there it was – ground beneath his feet. Beautiful, solid, dammitall Mother Earth. Jerry crawled out of the water and collapsed on the bank.

# 20

## *Hon-dah, Se-eh-ha*

*Fort Apache Reservation News*, June 4, 1946 // Council to Study Proposed Indian Medical Center // 5 Boys, 8 Girls Born at Whiteriver Health Service Hospital // Tribal Fair Queen To Be Chosen in August

The mud felt soft and comforting, as warm as the river was cold. Jerry lay unmoving and fought to keep from passing out. The feeling began to return to his arms and legs, and with it came the sting and pain of his cuts and abrasions. His limbs ached from exhaustion, and each arm and leg felt like it weighed a hundred pounds.

Jerry rolled over and sat up, trying to get his bearings. Straight ahead the piñon tree that saved his life remained in the water. The current roared over it, pounded it, determined to rid itself of anything that stood in its way. Had the current claimed Fan? Had she gotten out and, if so, where was she? Torn between hope and despair he told himself he'd rather she had drowned than be lying on the bank injured. The thought of having to put Fan down filled him with gut-wrenching fear. Jerry's heart sank.

Every movement was an effort, but he tugged off his heavy boots and poured the water out, mentally giving thanks that he hadn't tied them to Fan's saddle. Jerry stood up and stared back up the river and waited for his trembling legs to regain their strength. He had landed on a long stretch of narrow beach that ran along the base of the cliffs. Back across the river the sheer canyon walls rose hundreds of feet straight up from the water's edge – no beach, no chance of escape. He whispered thanks heavenward and began to walk.

Jerry had no idea how long he had been in the water. He'd put his watch in the tin on Fan's saddle. Wherever that might be. The sun beat straight down; it should be about noon, he thought. Jerry started walking, expecting at any moment to run out of beach. It continued, so narrow at times that his boots filled with water. The beach disappeared altogether two or three times and he had to scramble over boulders or hang onto bushes until he found another stretch of sand. He searched for any clue that Fan had made it out of the river but saw nothing.

Everything looked familiar. With each step came a sinking feeling and finally panic. He felt dizzy and disoriented. Could he have passed the spot where they entered? Jerry started to run. The bank curved, the beach widened and there they were – Fan's hoof prints leading out of the river. "She made it!" he shouted above the river's roar, his voice echoing off the canyon walls. Jerry dropped to his knees and examined the prints. They gave no evidence of a limp or an injury. Their depth in the sand told Jerry that she had stood there for a while. "You waited for me. Where are you, Fan?" He looked around. Alone and scared, she could be halfway to Phoenix by now. Jerry struggled to his feet and followed her prints to the base of the canyon wall. Fan had found a trail; her prints disappeared a few feet up the steep path.

Exhausted, cut and bleeding, and without food or the means to get it, Jerry fully appreciated his predicament. He stood for a moment gathering strength. His overriding thought – the fact that Fan had made it out alive. With an escape, a path leading up from the river, they still had a chance. Fan had taken that path and he intended to find her.

Not wanting to spoil his momentary good feeling Jerry dreaded looking up. When he did he sucked in his breath. The cliff rose eight hundred feet at least, maybe more. Looking back across the river at the sheer vertical walls he exhaled a sigh of resignation. The path might be steep but it would get him out of the canyon and away from the river.

The hot sun beat down, radiating heat off the rock wall and heating the air he breathed. Jerry scrambled up the narrow, precipitous trail. Every few minutes he had to stop and catch his breath and let his heartbeat slow. He refused to think about rattlesnakes, about muscles that screamed from exertion, or about how much his leg hurt. It had started to bleed again through the layer of mud that covered it. He fantasized that Fan would be at the top waiting for him. All he had to do was put one foot in front of the other.

Hours later, when Jerry heaved himself up the last couple of feet of the trail and onto flat ground, he couldn't straighten up. Gasping for air and still grunting from the exertion, he remained bent over with his eyes closed, hands on his thighs. When he could finally stand up straight and look around no pinto mare stood patiently waiting for him. Instead he saw half the state of Arizona stretched out before him.

The sun's position told Jerry that it was after four o'clock and that he faced southwest. To his right a broad alluvial plain sloped up to strange-shaped pinnacles and domed rocks, volcanic remnants the elements had carved into mysterious forms like the ones in the Palo Duro. To his left terraces and tiers of jagged cliffs led up to higher barren-looking slopes. An occasional tree interrupted the horizon and provided depth – visible markers of the magnitude of the plain.

He squinted at the skyline, for a moment thinking he was seeing a mirage. Jerry blinked and squinted harder – no mirage. In the distance under one of the trees he saw two figures and three horses. Instinctively he headed toward them. "God, I hope one of those horses is Fan and I pray whoever you people are, you're friendly," he said in their direction.

Jerry's mind tumbled with questions and possibilities. Were they prospectors, gun-toting treasure hunters, or desperados against whom he had no chance? According to the map the Lost Dutchman mine was nearby, a mountain full of hidden gold that every unhinged tourist and adventurous Ar-

116

izonan had dreamed of finding. Jerry wondered what they would think of him with one jeans leg gone, his exposed leg caked with mud and blood. Less than half of his shirt had survived. Its remnants hung open, unable to hide the cuts and scratches from the tree that had saved his life.

On foot with an empty holster and everything he owned on Fan, Jerry approached the figures with trembling legs and a knot in his stomach. As he drew close he saw that the two figures were young Apache men. Their horses were tethered to a paloverde tree. And the best sight he'd seen since spotting Fan's hoof prints in the sand was Fan herself. Jerry's heart skipped a beat. She looked perfectly fine. Fan looked up and nickered in his direction.

Camped in the shade of the tree, the campers' dwindling fire and empty spit told him they had been there for a while. Dressed like the young men he had seen on the way to Cibecue, they wore fringed leather pants and vests over their bare chests. One of them had pulled his long black hair straight back in a pony tail and tied it with leather; the other parted his hair in the middle and had two long braids that hung down his back. They were both gnawing on a leg of game that looked like jackrabbit. Jerry's empty stomach wrenched tighter at the sight and aroma of food. He spotted his Winchester on the ground between them next to Fan's saddle. She looked unconcerned, happy even. Standing in the shade with the two other horses she was nibbling at the withers of a handsome Appaloosa.

Jerry knew he couldn't win if he had to fight. Like crossing the Salt River this was another roll of the dice, a crap shoot. He took a deep breath, planted a smile on his face, and stopped on the other side of their fire. Standing as steady as his wobbly legs would allow he raised his right hand in a gesture he hoped looked friendly. He greeted them. "Hello. I've come from the land of *Tsa-La-Gi* – the Cherokee."

Black eyes set in bronze, implacable faces stared back at him. They said nothing. *They must not speak English.* Jerry

117

tried again. This time he made a fist and touched his heart then pointed at Fan. "Thank you for finding horse. I . . . me . . . very happy."

The Apache with the braids tossed aside the sucked-clean bone and looked at his friend. They spoke a few words. The second Apache laughed softly and said something back. Both men stood up at the same time. Jerry straightened, his eyes searching their faces for a clue of what they were going to do.

The Apache with the ponytail spoke. "*Hon-dah, se-eh-ha.* That is, 'welcome, elder brother' in our language. Your English is very bad for a white man." His greeting did not include a smile, but his voice held no threat and it echoed the soft guttural cadence Jerry had heard at Cibecue. Jerry stood on the other side of their fire, a glimmer of hope forming.

"Two Braids" gestured at the landscape. "You are lucky we find your mare. She would soon be buzzard meat out here."

The realization that they meant him no harm, combined with his hunger, the heat, and his exhaustion, took away whatever had held Jerry upright. Drained of all energy he sagged to his knees and then sat all the way down. "I'd be buzzard bait, too. I am all in. That was a helluva walk up the trail from the river." He could only whisper; he felt dizzy and lightheaded.

"You look bad, like you lost more than the mare. You have a fight?" "Ponytail" asked.

"Yeah, I fought the river and it almost won. That's how we got separated." Jerry nodded toward Fan. He gingerly touched his leg. "This happened when we slid down the top part of the trail on the other side of the canyon."

"The river is running full now, not a good time to cross," Two Braids said. "Your leg looks bad. You need medicine."

"I looked for a better place to cross but I couldn't find one. And we've come too far to turn around now. Fan and I started out in Oklahoma. We're on our way to Hollywood, California. My name is Jerry Van Meter."

118

The men spoke rapidly to each other and then Two Braids addressed Jerry. "I am known as William." The one with the ponytail told Jerry he could call him Elias. "We see movies sometimes at Theodore Roosevelt School in Cibecue. You a movie star?" Elias wanted to know.

"No star of any kind," Jerry said. "Just a cowboy. I went through Cibecue and saw a little of the rodeo. I'm surprised you didn't see me. I kinda stuck out like a sore thumb."

William shook his head. "I didn't have time to look around. Too busy trying to hang on to a Brahma that didn't much like Apaches." He jerked his thumb in Elias' direction. "Elias did better bronc riding."

Jerry had ridden bulls and broncs in half a dozen rodeos in high school around Enid and Guthrie. When he told them how his first bronc had sent him airborne, William and Elias smiled for the first time. They offered Jerry the rest of their rabbit. Between bites Jerry told them about the trip, about Fan getting distemper, and the snowstorm he had encountered.

"No wonder you look bad. We are on our way back to Cibecue," Elias said. "You come with us. We will take you to our medicine man. His herbs can fix your leg."

"Buy some new clothes at trading post – cheap," William added, eyeing Jerry's tattered jeans. "We have to cross the river, but we know a place not so dangerous."

Jerry smiled and shook his head. "Thank you for the offer but I've got some stuff to put on my leg and I'm exhausted. I don't think I could make it across that river again even with you two carrying me." They nodded that they understood.

Jerry finished his food and slowly got to his feet. William untied Fan and brought her forward. Elias saddled her, then William picked up Jerry's Winchester and shoved it in the scabbard. "Fine rifle," he said. "You will need it. Game is good around here, plenty of jackrabbits, javelinas too." Elias handed over Fan's reins. Relieved and happy that she looked okay, Jerry wanted to throw his arms around her neck. Instead he stroked her flank.

Jerry looked at the two men, his hand still on Fan. "Thank you, William. You, too, Elias. I'll always remember what you did. You saved my life."

"If you make a movie in Hollywood, make sure this time Indians win," William said, and shot a quick grin at Elias. "We don't like John Wayne movies. Indians are always bad. They scare even us." Jerry couldn't suppress his smile.

Rolla had insisted that Jerry carry silver dollars – for emergencies, he had told him. The Salt River certainly qualified, Jerry thought. He handed a coin to each of them.

"Is not necessary you pay. We – "

"This is a gift from a friend, not pay. Please. I want you to have them."

"Our custom is if you give a gift, then we must also and we have nothing," Elias said. William nodded.

"You gave me back my horse and all my things. You shared your lunch. Those are gifts. My gift is much smaller." William and Elias looked at each other and back at Jerry, then nodded their acceptance. He fished out his writing pad then wrote down their names in care of the Cibecue Trading Post, Fort Apache Indian Reservation, Arizona. They asked if he would send them a picture of movieland. Jerry promised he would, then mounted up and headed Fan toward Phoenix.

In his first few minutes in the saddle Jerry became painfully aware of every muscle in his body. He ached from exhaustion and the strain of a steady eight-hundred-foot climb. He hurt from being battered by the river. He felt something else even more acutely – an awareness of the hundred different things that could have happened, the majority of them bad. That they had survived without serious injury, that he'd found Fan and they were once again on their way seemed no small miracle.

"Thank you, Lord. This can only be Your doing. Yours and two very fine Apaches."

The Salt Canyon and the river crossing had cost Jerry more than a shirt, a pair of jeans, and a couple of silver dollars. It cost precious time on a journey that had none to spare. Three days' ride from Phoenix, somewhere in the Superstition Mountains, the thought that he might not make it to Hollywood in time crossed Jerry's mind for the first time.

# 21

## The Mountain Lion

*The Arizona Republic*, June 5, 1946 // Phoenix War Plants Convert, Provide Peacetime Employment // Prisoner of War Club Hopes to Reach State's 250 Ex-Prisoners // Bullet Bob Feller Pitches 10th Victory for Cleveland

Late the next afternoon Jerry and Fan reached the base of Rockinstraw Mountain and headed for the huge Roosevelt Reservoir. Just west of the dam they caught a ferry, which took them across the string of lakes and saved a day's ride to reach the north shore. Jerry made camp on the north shore of Apache Lake near the Horse Mesa Dam just as the sun began its final descent. Hot, crusted with sweat, dirt, and blood, and weary to the bone, Jerry dismounted, his eyes drawn to the lake. After removing Fan's saddle, he dumped his holster, gun, clothes, and boots in a pile then walked straight into the lake. Fan needed no urging; she led the way.

The soothing blue waters of Apache Lake washed away their dirt and pain and the fatigue of a thousand road-weary miles. Fan submerged herself like a giant sea monster, with her head barely sticking out of the water, and then walked up on the shore and shook, only to turn around and walk back in. Jerry laughed at her. "Feels good, huh, girl?"

Jerry floated on his back and squinted at the deepening color of the sky and the sunset-tinted clouds. The following day would prove crucial; they had to reach Phoenix – which Jerry estimated to be thirty-five miles due west. Fan's shoes had to be replaced, and she needed a full day's rest. She needed a lot more than that, but one day was all they could spare. They had come a thousand miles in thirty-three days. Tired and sore, and tougher and wiser, Jerry knew the toughest obstacle of all lay ahead – the Mojave Desert.

They played in the water until hunger drove him out. Jerry dried Fan down and fed her. Exhausted, she ate her grain and grazed for a few minutes and then went to sleep. Jerry was worn out as well, too tired to hunt even though he could have had his pick of small game. He ate beans and leftover biscuits and a can of peaches for dessert – sustenance, not pleasure. A canyon wren in a nearby paloverde tree sang him a sweet song while he ate. Jerry made a pot of coffee and drank two quick cups, hoping it would relieve his fatigue.

Like the skies of New Mexico, the Arizona night sky sparkled with millions of stars and a bright moon. Jerry glanced in Fan's direction, unseen now because of the deepening darkness. *What a champ she is, such a big heart.* He thought of the barber's question: "Why are you risking your neck?" He wasn't only risking his neck; Jerry knew he was risking Fan's as well. One factor loomed larger each day until now it had become his overriding concern. Jerry hadn't given in to it until the Salt River incident.

The bet and his original plan – to travel light in a race against time – had been based on a ride the length of a trail drive. But when Rolla and Frank had made their drives they'd had a remuda of ten to twenty horses, depending on the number of cowboys on the drive. The wranglers switched mounts every day, and rarely, if ever, did a horse put in the kind of duty Fan was enduring. Their drives were easier on the horses because the pace was set by the herd, and consequently they covered fewer miles in a day. To be fair, Jerry should have brought another horse, if not two others, so that Fan would not have had to carry his weight day in and day out. She had the strength and stamina of five horses, but it wasn't fair to her. Fan could very well end up lame because of a bet. She needed to regain her strength and get over her soreness – the signs of strain were becoming too obvious to ignore. She didn't bother to roll in the dirt when she came out of the lake. A horse who loved to eat, lately Fan hadn't even grazed when she had the chance.

Jerry felt exhausted too. His whole body ached, pushed to its limit with no chance of rest. His fatigue aside, he couldn't sleep; he felt restless and the need to feel close to his family. Away from any city, with only the moon, the stars, and a sleeping horse for company, writing to them was the only way Jerry knew how. He got out his pencil and writing pad and addressed a letter to his mother, father, and brothers. He wrote about the beautiful country he had seen. He told them the Rocky Mountains were majestic enough to be the throne of God. Jerry did not mention desperados or stampeding mustangs, or nearly drowning in the Salt River. He didn't tell them how grateful he felt to be alive and still in one piece. He told them his feelings about the trip.

*I feel like this trip has changed me, made me look at everything differently. One thing for sure, I won't take simple things for granted any more – good food, neat smells, being clean, a soft bed, and having people around who love me. Every day brings a challenge, something I've never faced. There's no one to rely on but me, so I have to find a way to meet it. I understand now, Dad, why you have always stressed being strong and responsible. This is not a journey for quitters.*

Jerry wrote a sentence or two to each brother; the last part of the letter he addressed to his mother. He wrote "I love you, Mom," and then paused, realizing that at twenty years of age, except for a "Love, Jerry" on a Valentine or Mother's Day card he had never written those words to her before.

*I want to thank you, Mom, for urging me to take this ride, for teaching me the importance of being honest and standing for something. I've seen the results of that firsthand on this trip.*

Jerry underlined the last part, thinking about how honest William and Elias had been to return Fan, his Winchester, and all his belongings.

*I can picture you in the kitchen cooking dinner and lining the boys up to turn their hands over to prove they washed good. I hope the Elberta peaches on my favorite tree will still be ripe when I get back and that you'll make me a peach cobbler – I think I could eat the whole thing. Tell Dad I'll want some of his ice cream on top. I love you all.*

Just as Jerry started to sign the letter he heard a God-awful scream, followed by Fan's terrified whinny. The sound resonated off the rocks and echoed out over the water, raising the hair on the back of his neck and changing his fatigue to fight-readiness. He grabbed the Winchester, leapt to his feet, and took off running toward Fan, his letter falling forgotten on the sand.

Out away from the firelight, Jerry saw the mountain lion. Thirty feet away on a flat rock above Fan and silhouetted against the moon, a male lion stood: six feet long, a hundred-fifty pounds of lithe power, crouched and ready to spring. Fan was rearing and kicking wildly. The cat flattened his ears and growled, its mouth open wide, flashing powerful teeth. As Jerry approached the cat turned his massive head and, for a millisecond, locked his golden eyes on Jerry's. In that blink of an eye Jerry's world went into slow motion. He barely heard the low ominous snarl rattling in the back of the cat's throat or Fan's whinny. Jerry stood mesmerized with the cat's beauty and power and then it growled again. The sound jolted him to action; he fired two shots in the air. The cat leaped off the rock and disappeared into the night, leaving Jerry to stare after him. He fired another shot in the air for good measure.

Fan still fought her tether, wanting to escape from the enemy. Jerry dropped the rifle, holstered his Colt, and grabbed her rope with both hands. She was all right, scared but not harmed. "Easy, girl," he said. It took a full five minutes of soothing and Jerry's steady hand to calm her. She blew and snorted and stiffened her front legs, alert and ready to bolt. When she finally quieted Jerry coiled up the picket rope and brought her closer to the campfire on the other side of his bed-roll.

He spoke to her softly. "Tell you what, Fan, I'll read you my letter." Jerry looked around for the pages, but they were no-where to be found. "I thought I wrote a letter." Fan nickered softly, and Jerry stroked her muzzle, for a moment wondering if he had actually written a letter or just dreamed that he had. His boot found the broken pencil sticking out of the sand. "I did write a letter, a long one. The breeze must have blown it into the fire."

Jerry reloaded the Colt, put more wood on the fire, and then stretched out on his bedroll. The second he closed his eyes he saw the cat's golden eyes staring back at him. "If I live to be a hundred I'll never forget those eyes," he said to the stars. The Winchester lay across his lap, ready. Jerry swore not to sleep, knowing sadly that if the cat came back, he would have no choice but to kill it.

# 22

## Horse Sense

*The Arizona Republic,* June 6, 1946 // Black Marketing Thrives in Food-Pinched Nation // Chicago Housewives Chase Bread Trucks Shouting Bids // U.S. Farm Prices Reach Highest Levels Since 1920

Jerry now began the day half expecting a calamity. That way he figured if one didn't happen it was a bonus, and if it did, he'd be ready. He thought back to the cowboy who had posed atop Fan for the *Guthrie Daily Leader* the day before he left. Foreman of the Bar R, rodeo rider, proficient handler of horses, he had considered himself a cowboy. Jerry shook his head and smiled. *What a greenhorn I was then.*

After two dips in Apache lake, Fan seemed fresh when they left at sunup the next morning. It soon became obvious, however, that they now faced a new enemy – the heat. By the time they stopped for lunch, it had to be a hundred degrees or more. When he removed Fan's saddle steam rose off her soaked back. She rolled in the dirt to soothe her skin.

To the south across the reservoir system of lakes, the Superstition Mountains stood tall against the sky like ancient fortifications. A land of red-hued monoliths carved into strange, splendid shapes by the elements, the mountains also were home to giant saguaros – monuments in their own right – and fragrant desert flora. They teemed with javelinas, black-tailed jackrabbits, chukars, deer, and puma. To Jerry, the Superstition Mountains meant rugged terrain and daunting temperatures. He used the sun and his compass to navigate through and around sun-baked canyons north of the string of lakes. Picking up a path – a sheep trail of long ago, judging by the hoof prints and sparse vegetation – Jerry kept a lookout

127

for rattlers as Fan walked along at a steady pace. He hoped they'd soon be out of these hills and onto the flat, open desert where there would be a breeze, albeit a hot one.

Fan slowed and came to a stop. Red lights went off in Jerry's head. What now? He quickly dismounted and checked her. She didn't have any mucus, and her breathing sounded fine. Jerry knelt down and checked Fan's shoes. Finding nothing wrong he glanced around for other signs of potential trouble. "What's the matter, Fan?"

Up ahead the arroyo narrowed, but from what Jerry could see, it looked like it flared out again within a few feet. Horses did not have good depth perception; perhaps she felt unsure about the opening. The sheer walls reminded Jerry of the draw where the stampede happened, except this one was twice as high and much narrower. Could Fan be remembering that? Jerry walked ahead and checked; nothing appeared unusual.

The trail led straight to Phoenix. Following it they could easily reach the outskirts of the city by dusk. If they had to backtrack around Roosevelt Dam and follow the highway on the other side of the lakes, they would lose a whole day. They were less than a yard from entering the narrow opening. Jerry unrolled Fan's lead rope and walked through it, tugging on the rope for her to follow. "What is it, girl? Are you still spooked because of the cat?" She splayed her front legs and stood stiff and straight, refusing to budge. The blazing sun beat down and radiated off the rocks, searing both of them from all sides, broiling and baking them. He felt like they were in an oven; he was soaked with sweat, and Fan was completely lathered.

"Come on, don't be mule-headed. We've come through a half-a-dozen canyons like this. Don't do this to me, okay?"

No amount of pleading or tugging could get Fan to move, and Jerry began to lose patience. Nothing seemed out of the ordinary that he could see. He pulled himself back into the

128

saddle and listened again. Hearing nothing Jerry spurred Fan with the hand-tooled spurs he wore but had yet to use on the trip. "Giddyup, Fan. Come on. Don't be stubborn."

Fan lowered her head and shook it, whinnied and side-stepped, refusing to move. Jerry dug the spurs in harder. "Dammit, Fan, let's go." His voice slammed back at him off the walls and reverberated through the canyon. Fan whinnied and reared up. Caught by surprise, Jerry gripped her sides and hung on to keep from getting dumped out of the saddle.

Starting as a low rumble, small rocks began to rain down. A boulder cracked loose from the wall above and crashed onto the trail in front of them. Jerry hung on as Fan jerked back and whirled around; she took off in a full run. It took everything he could do to stop her once they reached a wide spot well away from the rockslide. "Whoa, girl. Come on, whoa." He reined her in. "Damn, you'd run all the way back to Oklahoma if I'd let you." Jerry brought her to a halt in the shade of a giant saguaro and turned her around.

He held Fan steady and watched as boulders and rocks cascaded down and red dust rose in a thick cloud. When it cleared the canyon entrance had disappeared, replaced by a pile of boulders twice as high as Fan. Jerry sat motionless in the saddle, staring at the rubble and listening as small rocks plinked down on the pile. He knew horses had a sixth sense, but this was the first evidence of it he had ever witnessed.

"You just saved our lives." He dismounted and checked Fan's flanks where he'd used the spurs. A bloody line showed where the spurs had broken her skin. "You knew something wasn't right, and I wouldn't listen." Jerry ran his fingers across the scrape. "I'm sorry, girl. I'd better put something on it. I don't want you any madder at me than you already are." Jerry fetched the Bag Balm and applied it to the scratches on both flanks. He removed the beautiful spurs and put them in his saddlebag. *Never again.*

They backtracked a mile; Jerry dismounted and then tied Fan to a paloverde tree. He climbed over and around rocks and cacti to the top of a rise, then spotted another arroyo that ran parallel to the blocked one they'd just left. He climbed back down and untied Fan, leading her a short distance until she settled down. As soon as he could see an opening back onto the trail he pulled himself into the saddle and let her determine whether it was safe to walk through. She evidently thought so, for she trotted through as though she had forgotten the rockslide altogether. It took another hour to get out of the hills and into the open desert.

Jerry and Fan rode west chasing the sun, finally reaching the outskirts of Phoenix just as it set. A huge stockyard on the northern edge of the city loomed right in front of them. Jerry rode between rows of tall pole barns into the cool dimness, until he found the office. The stockyard manager had been a cowboy once – a hundred pounds ago. A Texan, he said, out of Dallas. White-haired and with a full beard neatly trimmed, he reminded Jerry of pictures he'd seen of Bill Cody. The manager informed Jerry that the stockyard was part of the Maricopa County rodeo circuit. Its restrooms and showers were for rodeo participants who did just what Jerry intended to do: stay with his horse.

"Y'all are welcome to stay as long as you need. The hay ain't moldy and the water's pure. You just passin' through?"

"You might say that," Jerry said and then gave a short explanation of his journey and the bet. He desperately wanted a shower, some hot food, and a good night's sleep.

"Well, I've heard it all now. Ridin' halfway across the country on a bet." The manager pointed outside toward Fan. "You'd best take care of that horse first. Looks pretty worn out. Now I understand why. I'll have Tony bring you some hay and grain. Pay when you leave."

"Thank you. By the way, do you know a good place close by to eat?"

Jerry's question brought a roar of laughter from the manager and woke Fan. "You asked the right man." He patted his belly. "The Stockman just down the block. They got the biggest and best steaks in Phoenix."

As promised, Fan got her cool bath first. "You've earned this and a whole lot more." Jerry dried her down.

The stableman, like the fairgrounds caretaker in Clovis, looked and acted concerned about Fan. He brought her hay and grain. After she had eaten her fill he brushed her and fed her two apples when he learned they were her favorite treat. Jerry showered and put on his clean shirt. He brushed and reshaped his Stetson as best he could and chuckled at the teeth marks forever imprinted in the brim. Jerry gave the stableman a dollar to keep an eye on Fan and his gear. "Gracias, mi amigo. I will take good care of this very tired horse. Would you like me to show you the dormitory? We have bunks you could use."

"That's okay. After what Fan's been through, I'd rather stay close by. Besides, I forgot what a real bed feels like. I don't want to get spoiled."

Fan had become much more to Jerry than a means to get to California. They were in this together; they had saved each others' lives. Her well-being meant as much to him as his own. As soon as he saw Fan resting and felt confident that she was in good hands Jerry followed the manager's directions to the Stockman's Bar and Restaurant.

# 23

## The Birthday Party

*The Guthrie Daily Leader*, June 6, 1946 // Higher Grain Prices Mean Famine Relief Abroad, Less Meat for U.S. // Oklahoma Vets Get Trade & Ag Training in New Program // Alaskans Vote in Favor of Statehood

"Vearl, would you fetch the boys from the bunkhouse? Dad and Frank are here," Edna Van Meter said to her husband. She glanced out the window. Frank and her father got out of Rolla's Chevy truck and were laughing at something as they walked toward the house. Edna marveled at them. Rolla would turn seventy-six on June 8 – in two days. Frank's eighty-sixth birthday was coming up in October, and they still moved like young men. "They're going to ride together in heaven, those two," she said to Vearl as he left to get the boys.

"I smell some good fried chicken," Frank said when he came through the door.

"If you want some you'll have to check your hat and guns at the door, cowboy." Edna gave them both a kiss on the cheek. She noted they were both spiffied up, as Rolla called it, and she smiled an acknowledgment to her father. "Happy birthday, Dad."

"Thanks, Edna. Since it's my birthday it'd be fine with me if you didn't feed this varmint. He's been givin' me grief all day."

Frank took off his holster. "I'll put my guns in the car, Edna. Pay Rolla here no mind. He thinks he's smart because he's havin' a birthday. I told him I'm always gonna be older and smarter 'n him. You back me up on this."

Edna laughed. "I'm not getting in the line of fire between Rolla Goodnight and Pistol Pete. I'd be the one to end up full of holes."

"Me against slow-draw Goodnight?" Frank grinned in Rolla's direction. "Be right back." He closed the door on Rolla's indignant glance.

All the food on the table had come out of the Van Meter garden or from their flock of chickens: four fryers, twenty potatoes mashed with homemade butter and cream, and four quarts of canned green beans from the victory garden. Edna, Vearl, and the boys raised chickens and sold them along with fresh eggs to the stores in Guthrie. Their large garden and five-acre orchard produced enough vegetables and fruits to feed their five boys and fill the cellar every winter. They shared their bounty with neighbors and during the summer made extra money from a roadside stand. During the Depression, Edna gave away more food than she sold.

After dinner Vearl helped Edna serve the birthday cake.

"Tell us the tarantula story, Grandpa," Bill said. Conversation stopped, and Bill, David, and Byron leaned forward in anticipation.

Rolla and Frank grinned at each other, about to tell one of their favorite trail stories. Rolla started. "Well, Frank 'n me had our hands full. We was drivin' this herd of longhorns along a dry riverbed. Everything seemed to be going fine when all of a sudden the poundin' of the cattle's hooves made all these tarantulas come to the top of the sand and start crawlin' up them longhorns' legs."

"Whooee," Frank said. "Them cows went crazy, jumpin' and kickin'. Next thing we knew they started stampedin'. We thought the herd was going to end up in Mexico before we could stop 'em."

"How did you stop them?" David said.

Rolla laughed. "Why, expert-like, of course. We – "

The telephone rang in the middle of the rescue. Edna got up and answered it. "Yes, I'll accept the charges." The excitement in her voice quieted the others. "It's Jerry. He's calling collect from Arizona."

Jerry watched patrons file in and out of the Stockman's Bar and Restaurant as the operator put through his call and asked his mother to accept the charges. "Jerry, it's wonderful to hear your voice. Where are you?"

"I'm in Phoenix, Mom. It's wonderful to hear you, too. Sounds like a houseful. Who's there?"

"Everybody but you and your brother Jimmy. We're celebrating Dad's birthday. It's actually this Saturday, you know. He and Frank are here for dinner. We were just having birthday cake. You couldn't have called at a better time."

Jerry closed his eyes. "What kind of cake?"

His mother chuckled. "Chocolate, the moist one I make with mayonnaise. It's so good to talk to you, son. I wish you were here."

"So do I." Jerry could almost taste the cake. "I feel terrible, Mom. I forgot about Grandpa's birthday."

"Don't worry. Hearing from you is the perfect gift."

Jerry talked to every member of his family, the longest long distance call he'd ever made. Rolla got on the line and asked if the wild china trees had leafed out yet in the Palo Duro when Jerry was there. Jerry told him they had and he heard his grandfather sigh. "Happy birthday, Grandpa. Wish I could celebrate with you."

"I appreciate that, son. You havin' a good time on your adventure?" Rolla didn't talk on a telephone very often, so when he did he felt it necessary to shout. Jerry held the phone away from his ear.

"I am, Grandpa, certain times more than others. I made it into Phoenix this evening. We're going to rest up all day tomorrow then head out over the desert on Saturday."

"Fancy's okay now? You need money? I know how to wire you some through Western Union."

"Yeah, Fan's fine, tired but fine, and I'm doing okay on money. Those silver dollars you had me bring along came in handy. Glad you told me to do that."

134

"We sure enjoyed your letter. Write us another one if you can. Before I forget, I ran into your friend Carlton Schier in Marshall the other day. He said to tell you he's rootin' for you. Wait a minute, Frank is grabbin' the telephone away from me, the old fart. I'm either gonna have to let him talk to you or shoot him."

Jerry pushed his hat back, shaking with silent laughter at the two of them. Noise followed in the background. Finally Frank's voice came on the line. "Thanks for the book, Jerry. I started readin' it the next day. Now tell me, did you really say that? Fill your hand, you son of a – "

"I did. It came out natural as can be. How you doin', Frank?"

"Well, I'll be dawg. I'm spit-fire fine, Jerry, and plenty proud of you."

Frank wanted to hear all about Fan. Jerry told him about the rockslide and how she had sensed it. "I knew she'd do right by you. I'm glad you're makin' the trip on her. She's got horse sense."

"Right this minute I'm thinking she's got more than me. You and Grandpa gonna stay in Guthrie tonight?"

"Yeah, your Mama talked us into it. The boys want me to listen to the 'Cisco Kid' with 'em on the radio. After that 'Roy Rogers and Dale Evans' is on with that Gabby Hayes fella. The boys say he's tryin' to imitate me. I told 'em slim chance."

Jerry asked to speak to his mother again before he hung up. "I wrote you a long letter but . . . I got sidetracked by something and it blew into the fire."

"What a shame. I would have liked that. Are you all right, Jerry? You sound tired."

"I am a little tired but we're going to rest up tomorrow. This country is really something, Mom. I'll try to write while I'm here so you'll get it next week."

Jerry could not bring himself to say aloud the things he had put in the letter. After he reluctantly hung up, he stood for a long time looking at the telephone, hating to break the connection to the people he loved most. The call buoyed his spirits

135

but at the same time brought on an acute attack of loneliness. Jerry could close his eyes and picture everyone sitting around the big table in the Guthrie kitchen. He could smell the fried chicken and chocolate cake and hear the laughter.

He bought the biggest steak on the menu from a pretty waitress who called him "cowboy" when she told him to sit anywhere he liked. "Want anything to drink with that steak?"

"I want the tallest, coldest beer you've got."

Every time she went by Jerry's table she stopped and visited, asking where he was from, finding out a little more about him with each stop. When Jerry mentioned a few of his adventures, she made him promise to tell her his story from the beginning. On her next stop she delivered a huge green salad smothered in buttermilk dressing. "My name is Sheila, and from the sounds of it you haven't had one of these in a while. It's on the house, except you have to tell me your name and why you're making this ride. I have a few minutes."

"Jerry Van Meter, from Guthrie, Oklahoma." He tore through the salad; it tasted as good as the steak. Talking between bites he told her about the bet and the journey. Sheila listened attentively and stayed until he finished his dinner. "Thanks for the salad and the company," Jerry said as he got up to leave. He left a silver dollar on the table.

"Anytime." She followed him to the door. "Hope you'll come back, Jerry."

Jerry bought four shoes for Fan on his way back to the stockyards. The next morning, with the stableman's help, they trimmed and cleaned Fan's hooves and replaced her worn shoes. Jerry watered and fed her, and she fell asleep again within a few minutes. "She es muy consado, señor, very tired indeed."

"So am I, but I've got some shopping to do before I sleep and I'd like to see a little of this city."

Jerry took a bus into downtown Phoenix. The stockyards were on the northernmost edge of the city, so the ride gave him an opportunity to see the contrast in landscapes. He passed acres of tiny box-like homes, businesses fronting on traffic-filled streets, then more homes and more businesses – a sprawling collection of districts and neighborhoods strung together by lanes of asphalt over what, not long ago, had been open desert. Phoenix stretched outward, gobbling up landscape from a busy nucleus that itself was very old. Bustling even in the midday heat, the city seemed to possess an energy: traffic and people, busy stores, businessmen with briefcases, shoppers walking along, their arms laden with packages. Rolla had told him that Jimmy Wakely predicted exactly this scene – booming cities and dying farms and ranches.

Signs of the war still showed: war posters, men and women in uniform, and war movies playing at the theaters. Jerry had to stare at how civilian women dressed – not in dresses but in long pants with military tops. He strolled along and looked in department store windows. Female mannequins dressed the same way: sloppy joe sweaters or military-looking jackets with epaulets. He wondered when anyone would ever need a jacket in Phoenix. His mother would never wear slacks. Trim, always properly dressed (as she called it), Edna considered a hat and gloves necessary attire when going out. The thought of her in slacks made Jerry smile. Men's suits looked like the civilian version of their military counterpart: double-breasted jacket, full pants with cuffs, and, at thirty dollars, almost a week's wages.

Jerry bought a new pair of Denim Riders and then stopped for an uptown lunch. He took a seat at the bar, ordered another salad with buttermilk dressing, and hoped it would be as good as the one he had at the Stockman's Bar. The radio behind the bar had Bill Stern on, interviewing Cleveland's star pitcher, Bob Feller. The bartender turned up the volume so Jerry could listen. By the time Jerry had finished his salad, Stern had finished the interview. "Bob Feller, what a guy," the bartender said. "Enlisted in the navy at the height of his career, highly decorated, you know."

"I know." Jerry knew all about Bob Feller, his brother Billy's hero. Billy collected pictures and newspaper clippings of Feller in his navy uniform as an antiaircraft gunner on the *U.S.S. Alabama*. His favorite picture was of Feller in his Cleveland uniform when he had joined the team as the youngest player in Cleveland's history. Billy wanted to be a major league baseball pitcher; at the very least he wanted to see Feller pitch now that Feller had returned to Cleveland.

"Yeah, quite a guy," Jerry said and paid his bill.

Bob Feller made him think of the navy. Riding the bus back north, Jerry wondered about his squadron. Where were his buddies now? What were they flying? It had been a long time since he'd thought about them or the navy.

When Jerry returned to the stockyards and walked up to Fan's stall, he found her still asleep. He could hardly keep his own eyes open, but he kept his promise. Jerry wrote letters to his family. His mother had scolded him for not telling her everything. Frank and Rolla must have shared their letter. This time Jerry wrote about the bad parts as well as the good: the rockslide and how scared he'd been in the Salt River when he got separated from Fan. He described meeting William and Elias and told her how they had helped him.

After finishing his letters, Jerry slept until hunger awakened him. He gravitated back to the Stockman's Bar and Restaurant – whether it was for the excellent food or the pretty waitress, he wasn't sure. Sheila greeted him with a dazzling smile. She wore her dark hair cut very short and curly – different from the women he knew in Oklahoma, a big city look he decided. It seemed every woman in downtown Phoenix had that same hairdo, and on Sheila it looked good. Friday night turned out to be quarter-drink night for anyone in the military or just out of the service, which pretty much took in all the men and women in the place.

The jukebox blared out one hit after another and after a month of silence, the music and laughter sounded good. Somebody must have really liked the Andrews Sisters' "Don't Sit under the Apple Tree" because it played three times in a row. The only bad part about it being so crowded was that Sheila didn't have time to visit. She did remember the salad, though. By ten o'clock every barstool was occupied, and a dozen couples danced, jitterbugging one minute then dancing to a sad cowboy song the next. Jerry stayed around until the crowd thinned. Sheila approached his table.

"I'm glad you stuck around. I hate that I've been so busy we haven't gotten a chance to talk. Didn't you tell me you were leaving tomorrow?"

"Before daylight in the morning. I'm kind of worried about the heat."

"I wish you didn't have to go so soon. I work the late shift tomorrow so I don't have to come in until five." She looked at him invitingly.

Jerry's heart sank. He knew without giving it a second thought that he couldn't stay. If he tried his hardest and didn't make it, at least he'd have given it his all. If he stayed to spend the day with a pretty girl and didn't make it, he would never forgive himself. "I'd like nothing better, but I can't."

"I understand. But you can do one thing for me before you go. You can dance with me."

"It's been a long time since I danced – " Jerry started to make excuses and then realized what he was turning down. "Yes, ma'am," he said.

She led him onto the empty dance floor. Jerry put a nickel in the jukebox. "Pick whatever song you want."

She chose "Somebody Else is Taking My Place." They danced, oblivious to the small crowd that watched them. Sheila put both arms around Jerry's neck and sighed contentedly with her cheek against his. When the song finished, Sheila kissed Jerry good-bye. It made leaving all that much harder.

139

## Mother Nature's Frying Pan

*The Wickenburg Sun*, June 9, 1946 // Boy Scouts Collect Canned Goods for Starving Europeans // Strict Measures Result from Arizona's Worst Drought Since 1921 // May and June Precipitation Zero, Temperatures Reach 106

Jerry and Fan rode out of Phoenix before dawn on June 9, headed for the Colorado River and California. The stableman, when he'd said good-bye the previous night, suggested they find shade in the hottest part of the day and travel as much as they could before daylight and after sunset. Common sense told Jerry to follow that advice.

The homes on the northern fringe of the sprawling city looked like small, rectangular brick boxes with low roofs and shallow yards. *Hot*, Jerry thought as he rode by. Moonlight glinted off their silent dark windows, opened to catch the desert breeze. A few vigilant dogs barked at the shadowy intruders. A lone porch light went on, then off, and the neighborhood became quiet and dark once again. Jerry and Fan reached the open desert hours before the sun came up. Not long after it rose he realized the stableman's suggestion would be difficult to follow.

Shade, in the form of mesquite trees and bushes, could rarely be found. And shade or no shade, the unrelenting heat enveloped them like a blanket. It rose off the desert floor in shimmering waves, baking them from beneath and searing them from above, the air so hot it seemed to cook from within. By the time they stopped for their first rest at eight A.M., Fan was completely lathered, and Jerry was soaking wet. The early sun's rays came from behind him, but its glare bounced off the sand, blinding like sun on snow. He thought about his crumpled discarded Stetson; Fan would look ridiculous with it on her head, but he wished he had saved it for her anyway.

Their first evening out brought a gift, a cloud cover that blocked the sun and created huge patches of shade on the parched earth. Thunderheads began to form as Jerry and Fan approached the Hassayampa River south of Wickenburg. The riverbed's gouged-out banks spoke of past storms and raging torrents, but now it had barely enough water for desert creatures to survive. After thirty miles in suffocating heat, Jerry decided to make camp. The storm held the promise of rain, and the stableman had warned that Arizona rainstorms created instant torrents in washes and riverbeds.

Dismounting near a group of mesquite trees close to the river, Jerry unpacked, keeping his eye on the intensifying storm. The wind picked up as the sky darkened. Thunder rumbled, and flashes of lightning streaked through the black clouds. With the blinding sun hidden, the desert's colors brightened and its fragrance came to life. A trio of prairie dogs near the river's bank stood at attention, waiting expectantly.

Jerry felt his skin cool and his lungs expand with moisture-laden air. Lightning flashed, and Jerry, Fan, and their prairie dog neighbors were treated to an all-encompassing cloudburst. A lengthy deluge, the downpour swelled the water level in the river, and Jerry had to scramble to replace Fan's bridle with a halter as she determinedly headed into the stream.

There were at least two givens about Fan: her endless appetite and her love of water. Many times in Oklahoma when Jerry had been riding her and she spied a body of water, she had headed into it undeterred by his objections. This river proved to be no exception: she waded right in and began to drink. If she drank slowly, Fan could take in five gallons at one time without foundering. She did exactly that – drank slowly – though their ride had been long and hot.

Her crisp brown and white colors brightened after Jerry waded in and washed the crusted sweat from her coat. She stretched her neck and shook as he scooped the cool water over her – a sign she liked it. Fan stayed in the river a long time, and when she came out, she rolled in the dirt, first on one side and then on the other. Afterward she looked as dirty as she had before the storm.

"You look terrible." Fan stared back at him, chomping contentedly on the rolled oats he had put in front of her. Jerry chuckled at her happy face: thirst-quenched, cool, dirt-covered, and eating. "Frank was right, you are one great horse."

By the time Jerry cleaned himself up in the river, the storm had rumbled past and Fan was asleep. She had become a savvy traveler, eating and drinking when offered, seeking out the little bit of shade when it could be found, and sleeping at the first opportunity. The storm provided plentiful water for Jerry to refill his containers and to wash his sweat-soaked clothes and Fan's blanket. Everything had faded from being washed so often and dried in the bright sun.

The next morning the heat returned, but for a short while the desert and everything in it felt and looked refreshed. The moist sand lent an earthy fragrance to the morning; the air crackled with freshness. Jerry breathed deep with enjoyment, but both pleasures were short-lived, only lasting until the sun came up.

Jerry and Fan skirted the base of the Big Horn Mountains, mesquite-covered hills that rose abruptly from the flat desert expanse. At the end of their second day, ten miles east of Quartzsite, they intersected Highway 10. Jerry couldn't resist looking back at the two lanes of asphalt. It narrowed with the distance into a shimmering thread, finally becoming no more than a speck on the horizon. Jerry patted Fan's wet neck. "Look how far we've come."

Cars, with canvas water bags hanging by thick rope from door handles or as hood ornaments, rumbled by on the highway. Most of the drivers honked a greeting, and then Jerry would see hands appear through open windows to wave. Without fail, every head in every car turned to stare, curious at what a horse and rider would be doing in the middle of this God-forsaken landscape. Several cars stopped, and people offered water and asked if they could help. Jerry accepted the water, not bothering to explain their presence. If he had told them they would have thought he was crazy. *Maybe I am.*

The town of Quartzsite consisted of an intersection of two ribbons of asphalt that came out of nowhere, met in the middle of nowhere, and then stretched into nowhere in all four directions. Businesses on two of the corners and a few attendant shacks provided the only sign that life existed at this crossroads. Quartzsite and its surroundings, Jerry thought, made the Texas panhandle look like a park.

The farther west they rode, the more desert-like and sparse the vegetation became. Ocotillo, creosote bushes, mesquite, chaparral, and prickly cacti stood as proud survivors of the heat and meager rainfall. Jerry thought back to the beginning of the desert below the Mogollon Rim, with its mild temperatures, plenty of water, and shade. Those were aberrations for something called a desert. *This* was the desert he dreaded when he'd planned the trip – landscape that threatened to bake the life out of anyone or anything with the audacity to try and cross it.

The body reacted to extreme heat by sweating profusely to cool itself. It meant that Fan stayed soaking wet all the time, and Jerry did too. He recognized the symptoms: cramping muscles, fatigue, and limbs that felt like lead. Jerry made a point to eat salt every morning and began adding it to Fan's food every other day. Instead of three rests per day, he upped it to four. He knew the sweat-soaked saddle blanket against her back, combined with the tremendous heat, invited trouble. Each time they stopped he took her saddle off and dried her back with a towel. He fed Fan sparingly, but often, and did the same with water. It was important to keep the tissues of her mouth moist. As miserable as conditions were, when they camped after the sun went down she always rolled like a puppy in the dirt – a good sign.

They started each morning well before dawn and traveled long after the sun went down. If Jerry could find shade in the hottest part of the day, they stopped and slept, then rode again until they were too tired to ride any more. The nights cooled off only slightly, ten to twelve degrees less than the one-hundred-degree-plus days, but the absence of the blinding sun made it seem cooler.

Late in the afternoon of their fourth day out of Phoenix, Jerry and Fan reached the Colorado River. Ehrenberg, Arizona, occupied the east side of the state line, and Blythe, California, the west. Jerry felt an overwhelming sense of accomplishment as he rode toward the Agricultural Inspection Station sign at Ehrenberg. It was day forty and they were 1245 miles from Guthrie. They had ten days to cover the 255 miles to Hollywood. Heat, fatigue, sweat, and hunger – his constant companions for the last few weeks – disappeared, swept away by a rush of pride. They had crossed two states and part of two others. They had made it to California's doorstep.

"Look at that, Fan. Hollywood, here we come. We'll follow the highway from here on in and be there in plenty of time." Fan's ears didn't twitch or move. Jerry squeezed her with his knees. "Hey, you awake?" She flicked her ears a couple of times. "That's more like it."

Up ahead a sign that said "Welcome to California" hung from the side of the closest building. In the adjacent parking lot, a half-dozen 1941 Packards were lined up diagonally, side by side, in a black and white display of authority. Black in the front and rear with white roof and mid-section, each car had a California Highway Patrol seal painted in the middle of the doors and a spotlight near the driver's window. Huge diesel rigs were also parked in the lot. Jerry could see uniformed CHP officers moving silently around the trucks checking tires

144

and brakes. When he saw their pistols and wide belts lined with bullets, his smile vanished.

He stopped in front of a uniformed guard, who was as wide as he was tall, sitting in the shade of the building with the welcome sign. The expression on his face was anything but welcoming as he stood up and signaled for Jerry to dismount.. The guard spoke in an officious tone, and his words matched his demeanor. "And just where do you think you're going on that horse, mister?"

Jerry moved himself and Fan into the shade from the building. "We're on our way to Hollywood . . . sir."

"Not on a horse you're not."

Jerry's heart sank. "What do you mean? I don't understand."

"If you'd paid attention to the signs along the highway you wouldn't have to ask."

"We came across the desert, didn't reach the highway until Quar – "

"At the present time an interdiction is in effect that bans bringing horses into the state of California." He spoke in an exasperated sing-song voice.

Jerry wondered what kind of problem they'd had and how widespread it could be to prompt such a ban. The guard rattled off the name of a disease, and, deep in thought, Jerry didn't catch it. It didn't sound like anything he had ever heard of, but he wasn't about to ask the guard to repeat it. He needed to know how long this interdiction would last. "Exactly what does that mean, 'at the present time?' Is it just today or this week?"

The guard smirked. "It means there's no way you're going to cross *this* border on *that* horse. And it's not going to be over in the next few days or weeks." He took a long look at Fan. Jerry's eyes followed his gaze. Her head hung low and her eyes were half-closed; the exhausted mare had fallen asleep. *He thinks she's sick.*

145

"You'd better go back where you came from, mister. And don't even think of sneaking across. If they catch you," he glanced at the CHP officers, "they'll impound your horse and quarantine it. Who knows when or if you'd ever get it back." The guard stared, his arms folded over his stomach. "Well?"

"Thanks for letting me know," Jerry said, trying not to let his anger show. With his jaw clinched tight, he pulled himself back into the saddle and turned Fan around. "What a grump. Sure as hell the wrong guy to put under a nice thing like a welcome sign, unless they put him in Quartzsite." The thought made him smile.

When they came to Main Street, Jerry spied a dusty little grocery store. A huge sycamore tree stood beside the building and cast some inviting shade over the sidewalk and the weed-covered lot next door. Fan headed for the shade automatically. Jerry wrapped her lead rope around the tree trunk and removed her saddle. "*Now* what do I do?" He leaned against the tree, the guard's words ringing in his ears: "you're not crossing this border on that horse." But in his mind Jerry pictured Rolla and Jimmy shaking hands, Frank handing him his Colt, and Highway 10 out of Quartzsite stretching all the way back to Oklahoma.

Fan had begun eating dry grass. "If I cross the border, I'm breaking the law. If we get caught, I'll lose you, girl. I can't lose you, no matter what." Dispirited, Jerry left Fan and went into the store to buy supplies.

146

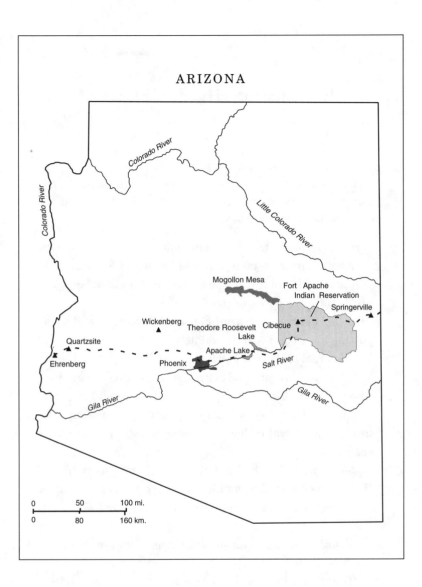

# ARIZONA

Colorado River

Colorado River

Little Colorado River

Mogollon Mesa

Fort Apache
Indian Reservation

Springerville

Wickenberg

Theodore Roosevelt
Lake

Cibecue

Quartzsite

Apache Lake

Ehrenberg

Phoenix

Salt River

Gila River

Gila River

| 0 | 50 | 100 mi. |
|---|---|---|
| 0 | 80 | 160 km. |

# 25

# Last Rest Stop for a Hundred Miles

*California Highway Patrolman Magazine*, June, 1946 // War Cost Equates to Building $8,000 House for Every U.S. Family // CHP Patrolmen Take Part in Police Traffic Safety Check // War Ends CHP's Responsibility for Japanese Relocation Camp Security

Jerry came out of the store twenty minutes later to find three boys between six and ten years old looking at Fan and whispering to each other. When he walked up, the oldest boy spoke up. "Is this your horse, mister?"

"Sure is," Jerry said. He put Fan's saddle back on and began putting his groceries in the saddlebags.

"It's a real pretty horse, what's its name?"

"The horse is a she, and her name is Fan. Do you boys have a horse?"

The youngest boy spoke up, displaying a missing front tooth. "I gotta schtick horse," he said, whistling through the space.

Jerry laughed. "I had a stick horse when I was your age." He retrieved a knife from his jeans pocket and cut an apple into wedges. "Want to help give her something she really likes?"

"Yeah," they said in unison and stepped forward. "Can I pet her?" the little one whispered.

"Hang on a minute. Let's give her the treat first." Jerry placed an apple wedge on each outstretched palm and showed them how to stiffen their fingers downward and together to keep them out of the way. The ten year old went first, giggling when Fan removed the apple from his hand. Fan ate the two other slices from upheld palms, and then all three youngsters wiped their hands down the sides of their pants. Each boy tentatively patted Fan's flank. Other than twitching her ears and tail, Fan paid no attention to the youngsters and ate the rest of her apple in peace.

"I'm gonna have me a horse like that when I grow up," the ten-year-old boasted. "Just like Fan."

Jerry finished his packing as the boys' mother came from across the street to retrieve them. She smiled at Jerry. "I hope they didn't bother you. They're crazy about horses. All they talk about is being cowboys. I'm sure they didn't expect to meet a *real cowboy* today."

Something in the way she said "real cowboy" – with a touch of admiration in her tone – made Jerry straighten up and stand taller. "No bother, my pleasure, ma'am." Jerry touched the brim of his Stetson and winked at the boys. "Bye, cowboys. Thanks for helping with Fan." Something about them reminded him of his brothers. They walked away with their mother, all chattering at once. Jerry heard the ten-year-old say "real cowboy" as he turned around and waved.

"Shoot, Fan, I don't want to quit now. We've come too far to not at least put our feet in California. How about it? What do you want?" Fan nudged his hand. "That's easy, you want more apple."

Jerry and Fan circled back through town, heading north and east away from the border crossing. At the northern edge of Ehrenberg Jerry turned west again toward the river. Tents and campers lined the banks of the Colorado. On the river side, in front of each camp, most campers had rigged some sort of makeshift canvas to nearby bushes and trees to provide shade. Under them they placed tables and chairs. In back of the tents, cars with license plates from Minnesota, Iowa, and Wisconsin sat covered with dust. Noisy children chased each other around and between the tents and cars, while their parents fished or sat in the shade visiting with neighbors.

Jerry kept riding for another hour until he saw no more campers and the river looked safe to cross. He guessed they had come about fifteen miles north of Ehrenberg.

The Colorado was a third the width of the Salt River and looked much less formidable. The water flowed by at a leisurely pace and it didn't look all that deep. Jerry tied everything on top of Fan's saddle once more and grabbed onto her tail. She waded in. As the cold water started filling his boots Jerry's heart sped up. "Here we go again. Let's do this one more time." Jerry was prepared for trouble, but no trouble came. He hung onto Fan's tail with his left hand and paddled with his right, this time crossing without incident. The harrowing experience of the Salt River seemed a long time ago.

Jerry looked back across the river. "Well, we made it into California, girl. Not exactly like I planned, but we're here." Jerry spoke quietly then looked around. "Why am I whispering? There isn't another person in sight." He knew why: the mental image of black and white patrol cars and armed patrolmen . . . *if you're caught your horse will be impounded.* The thought sent a shiver up his spine.

After he set up camp, Jerry led Fan back into the river. He cleaned her off and took a proper bath himself, then washed his clothes and draped them over a thick bush. With one-hundred-degree air they would dry easily by bedtime. In Phoenix Jerry had seen men wearing short plaid pants that reached just above the knee. He had snickered about it and asked the bartender where he'd eaten lunch just what the world was coming to – grown men wearing little-boy pants. "They're the latest thing," the bartender told him. "Called Bermuda shorts, and in this heat they aren't such a bad idea."

"I'm gonna make me a pair of Bermuda shorts, Fan." Jerry cut the remaining leg off his ruined jeans. She watched him put them on as she grazed near the water's edge. "I don't want any snickering on your part, lady. These jeans and my leg are what kept you from getting barely a scratch sliding down that mountain. Besides, now I'm right up to snuff."

150

He gave Fan her rolled oats and then walked along the shore, chuckling at how silly he must look in his cut-off jeans and cowboy boots. His leg had healed now with only a few scabs left to remind him of his quick trip down the Salt River Canyon trail. A few yards up from camp Jerry found what he was looking for – a boulder protruding into the river. Climbing out on the rock he held his makeshift fishing pole with one hand and slapped mosquitoes as fast as he could with the other. Two twelve-inch trout hung from Jerry's line in no time; he could have had a dozen more. The fish were in a feeding frenzy, biting at the pesky insects that landed on the water.

Though the sun had set, the air felt stifling. Fan did not roll in the dirt. She simply drank, ate, and went to sleep. "You look exhausted, Fan. Could you even make it across the desert?"

After his supper, Jerry cleaned his Colt and Winchester and organized his supplies, glancing at Fan as he worked. Disparate feelings – fear of the desert, compassion for Fan, desire to keep his word – all fought for recognition in his mind. At odds with those feelings were his core beliefs, everything Jerry had been taught and what he stood for. Emotional dilemma aside, he knew he had to make a decision.

He had planned to cross the desert following alongside Highway 10 into Palm Springs. Doing so would have given them a twofold safety factor: access to food and water at gas stations and grocery stores along the highway and help if they got into trouble. The interdiction made it a far greater challenge. If he decided to go on he chanced losing Fan to armed highway patrolmen with bullets on their belts. If they were to have a chance at winning now, it would come only if they faced the Mojave alone and headed straight across the desert.

Jerry didn't want to make a reckless decision, one based on pride simply because three little boys who reminded him of his brothers had called him a real cowboy. He stared into the darkness toward the desert. He knew the country behind them; he could only guess what lay ahead. He looked back

151

across the river, trying to get a gut feeling of what to do. It looked the same. "Okay, Fan," he said softly. "Just suppose I say the risk isn't worth it. Then what? How's it gonna be to actually turn around and ride back to Oklahoma? A hundred miles of desert ahead against twelve hundred miles back. How much worse could it be?"

The process of mentally following through on both alternatives gave Jerry his answer. Most important was that turning around meant giving up. Breaking the law or not, he could not go back. "This is not a journey for quitters." He had written that in a letter to his family, and within those seven words lay the crux of it.

Once he made that decision, Jerry decided something else. Weight and strength-wise, Fan had visibly lost ground, her feistiness was gone. At least it seemed to be absent on this blistering night. With temperatures during the day above one hundred degrees it would be asking the impossible for her to carry his one hundred seventy pounds across the desert. Jerry decided the only chance they had for making it would be for him to walk.

Between the realization of what lay ahead and the pesky insects that buzzed around him, Jerry slept little. At two A.M. it was as cool as it would be all day; he decided to quit trying. The sun would not be up for another four hours. Jerry led Fan to the river and made sure she drank her fill and then gave her a can of grain. He filled his gallon water container and the canvas bag he'd bought and ate his last two eggs.

# 26

## The Mojave

*California Highway Patrolman Magazine*, June, 1946 // Scalpers Sell Promise of 1946 New Car Delivery for Up To $300 // Tire Rationing Remains in Force, Supply Lags Demand // 35 MPH War Time Speed Limit Changed to 55 MPH

Setting a southwest course on his compass, Jerry angled straight across the desert. Following his plan, he walked for four hours at a comfortable stride then took a fifteen minute break. Far from Fan's eight-mile-an-hour pace, Jerry's was probably more like three, but he considered it progress nonetheless and easier on Fan. The bright moonlight filtering through the trees, cacti, and bushes cast eerie shadows on a landscape still unseen. Jerry thought about rattlesnakes but refused to worry about them. Just in case, though, he wrapped Fan's lead rope around his wrist and held it tightly in his hand.

Daylight broke between five-thirty and six, and the sun rose not long after. He dreaded its appearance and the minute it came up, he knew why – it felt like a hot iron against his shirt. And with the bright sun casting away the night, Jerry saw with crystal clarity what lay ahead.

The parched landscape stretched into infinity, the sight of it as daunting as the Salt River, the robbers, the mountain lion, and the Texas panhandle all rolled into one. His first full look made Jerry's knees weak. Dotted with prickly plants, the likes of which he'd never seen, this place was a world all its own. The sun's first rays were kind, but only for a moment. In the blink of an eye, the desert's vibrant colors bleached to a lifeless monotone, paled by the same sun intent on frying the two of them in Mother Nature's skillet called the Mojave Desert. Even the sky seemed stripped of its color.

The enormity of what he saw didn't change the pace or length of Jerry's stride. Instead, it triggered an automatic response to *not* pause, to *not* stop, to keep moving. Jerry had learned many lessons on this journey, and foremost was the importance of maintaining forward progress, however small that progress might be. They had made it over twelve hundred miles of tough terrain sticking to that plan. Each step brought Jerry and Fan closer to their destination, whether it had been to the top of the Continental Divide or to the edge of the Mogollon Rim. Whether lesson or survival instinct, Jerry didn't know, but he did not hesitate.

A closer look at the ground revealed iron-stained rocks scattered on top of or half-buried in the dirt. And depressions in the sand, their concave shapes white with salt or alkali residue, appeared as shallow dents in an otherwise flat desert floor. Unfriendly bushes with thorns and spikes demanded his constant attention to keep from running into them. Prickly pear, century cacti, creosote bushes, and scraggly mesquite stood like hardy soldiers, as at home in this inhospitable setting as the peach and plum trees were in the fertile soil of his Guthrie orchard. Jerry spotted the distinctive tracks of a sidewinder in the sand.

During his trip preparations Jerry had been warned that the air temperatures could reach one hundred twenty degrees during the day and the sand itself could go as high as one hundred fifty degrees. He distinctly remembered thinking that they would be across the desert before it got so hot. In the safe confines of the Bar R kitchen, it was impossible to envision this kind of heat or fathom that being wrong about it could cost them their lives. He surely couldn't be the only one who had ever miscalculated the desert's ferocity. Had others done the same? And if so, had they made it? Jerry remembered hearing stories about people suffering heat prostration. Who had told him those stories or when he had heard them he couldn't recall, and he didn't know exactly what the term "prostration" meant. But by noon that first day he began to get an inkling. Skin that burned like it was on fire, feeling light-headed and disoriented, and being thirsty down to the core of his being told Jerry he had discovered its meaning in spades.

Fan had tanked up in the Colorado River. Free of his weight and walking at a reasonable pace, she could go an entire day without drinking. Jerry gritted his teeth and vowed to do the same. Desert Center lay forty miles ahead; they had enough water to make it that far. Assuming he had set his compass accurately, they should come within a mile of it. He would tether Fan in a shady place out of sight and be in town only long enough to stock up on water and food. Jerry refused to plan any further than that.

Determined to keep moving, he walked through the first day with a fifteen-minute break every four hours. He kept saying aloud that they would be just fine, but his words were not what kept Jerry's fatigue at bay. Looking at what lay ahead and an all-encompassing fear spurred him onward. He willed away fatigue. The minute he felt signs of it Jerry fought it by picking up the pace. At each stop he gave Fan water from the canvas bag plus a handful or two of grain, and as soon as she was finished, they moved on. He did not remove her saddle because to do so would have doubled the time of each break. As long as they were moving forward they would be okay.

The sun finally set on their first day. Jerry stopped long enough to eat a can of pork and beans and drink a cup of water. He watered and fed Fan and for a moment thought how nice it would be to sleep. But the image of a slithering sidewinder spurred him to resume walking.

His pace had not changed the next morning when daylight arrived. With a total of two hours for breaks out of the previous twenty-eight since they'd left the Colorado River, Jerry figured they had easily covered forty miles. Since midnight he had kept an eye out for lights off to his left, but saw none. "We should have come right by Desert Center, Fan. What happened?"

Jerry scanned the morning horizon to the south – no sign of a town. Only endless desert, endless sky. He was afraid to turn south and walk to the highway – he didn't want to take the chance of running into the highway patrol. Equally fearing to veer from his SW heading and get off course, Jerry kept walking.

Morning flowed into the second afternoon without notice. Jerry willed himself to forget the sun searing from above and the heat boiling up from the sand. He concentrated on keeping a steady pace, counting an imaginary cadence in his head to keep focused. His step had undoubtedly slowed but the compass remained constant, which meant that as long as they kept moving they would intersect the highway at the next town: Indio.

As the day wore on it became more difficult to maintain his concentration. His mind kept drifting. Jerry relived the moment his commander told him his navy career was over; it seemed inconsequential now. He thought about his brothers at home, and his brother Jimmy – maybe in California, maybe in Guam. *Do they miss me? Does Jimmy even know I'm on this trip? Are Mom and Dad worried?* He imagined lavender perfume so clearly he could smell it and saw pretty Claire Elizabeth Dupree behind the counter of her daddy's store and dark-haired Sheila stopping by his table with a fresh salad and a dazzling smile. *That salad tasted so good.*

Jerry wondered if Charles Goodnight had ever been in a predicament like this. *This hot, this thirsty, this alone. What would a great man like him do? What would Grandpa and Frank do?* The miles, the vistas, the people, the hardships, and the funny moments mixed and twisted and swirled into a sun-baked montage. Jerry had to keep rousing himself back

156

to the present, to remember what day it was, to check his compass, and to look back and make sure Fan still followed behind.

Morbid thoughts crept into his mind even though he fought them. *If I had drowned in the Salt River or had been shot to death in New Mexico it would have been over quick. Out here it could be the heat, or running out of water, or a snakebite – anything could kill me. I'd have plenty of time to see it coming.*

The realization that death could come so easily gave Jerry a jolt. He tried to pick up his pace but Fan would not. She plodded along with her eyes half-closed, asleep on her feet. Jerry grew fearful that she would lie down and give up. Sometime during the night they had finished the water in the canvas bag. His gallon canteen was now all they had. "Keep moving or die, keep moving or die," he muttered in a sing-song voice under his breath.

To keep from drifting off and to make sure he maintained his compass heading, Jerry played a game. Using the sun's position and the length and angle of his shadow, he guessed the time and then checked it against his watch – the goal being to hit it exactly. The game required enough concentration and mental acuity to keep his focus for a few minutes so Jerry upped the ante, trying to guess the beginning of each hour.

That lasted until three o'clock when he started looking for shade. A scraggly mesquite bush about his height was all Jerry could find. He positioned Fan on the shady side then knelt in her shadow and poured two cups of water into his hat. Jerry scooped the water over Fan's face again and again, letting it fall back in the hat. Afterward he washed out the inside of her mouth with his hand. Keeping the tissues of her mouth moist was more important now than getting water into her stomach. An old cowboy who had been in the Foreign Legion in north Africa had told him that, but again he couldn't remember when or where. Jerry drank all the water that remained.

Dusk came. Blessed dusk. The sun sank below the horizon at the end of their second day, allowing Jerry's sun-burnt eyes to open instead of squint. Like an alarm clock the sun's disappearance signaled the desert coming to life. Field mice and lizards scooted out of his way, scorpions and tarantulas scuttled under rocks as he walked by. Jerry heard the sweet sound of birds singing and wondered where they hid during the day. A black-tailed jackrabbit bounded past, startling him with its energy. Jerry thought of the rabbit he'd eaten with William and Elias, and that reminded him how hungry he felt. He almost stepped on a tortoise that chose to withdraw into the safety of its shell when Jerry brushed it with his boot. The welcome presence of life, however minute or unrelated, lifted Jerry's spirits. It offered hope; it stirred him back to reality and forced aside the sun's mind-numbing stupor. Dusk was the best part of the day, when the sky changed to the gold of Oklahoma wheat fields, slid through layers of reds, oranges, and pinks, and settled at last into deep purple and the promise of night.

"We won't miss Indio, Fan. We missed Desert Center. Easy to do out here where everything looks the same. It'll be all right, girl. Don't worry, we're going to run right into Indio."

Jerry's gallon canteen could last another twenty-four hours if they drank only enough to moisten the tissues of their mouths. Indio was one hundred miles from the Colorado River. *If my heading is true it can't be more than twenty or thirty more miles. This time I can't afford to miss.*

Jerry walked through his second night and into the third day, cognizant only that they had passed from dark to light. Walking at half the speed of his first day, he didn't know for sure if he had slept while he walked but he suspected he had. Quickly checking his compass heading, Jerry looked back to make sure Fan was still there. The sight of her plodding along with one hoof in front of the other, seemingly unaware of the scorching earth, broke his heart. Jerry wondered if hooves burned like feet and if hers hurt. He could no longer feel the heat coming through his boots; he couldn't feel his feet at all.

Jerry's new size thirty-two Denim Riders, the ones he'd bought in Phoenix, slipped low on his hips. *It's okay, I'll gain it back*, he thought as he hitched them up. He avoided saying "if," though the nagging thought remained in the back of his mind. His eyes were scorched, and he could feel sores on his lips. His hair had grown long again, matted and stiff with sweat. He hadn't stopped to shave or brush his teeth since leaving the Colorado River. The shaving mirror remained in his pack; he wanted no reminder of how he looked.

Out of the corner of his eye Jerry spied something a few feet off to his right, a pile of bleached bones, a lost steer or maybe a mule. Still in the position in which it died, with each bone in place and undisturbed, he envisioned Fan looking that way if she lay down and gave up. Jerry glanced over his shoulder.

Fan's eyes did not open nor did her stride change. He called back to her in a raspy voice. "Do you have any idea how nice it's going to be when we get to Hollywood? It's pretty and green, lots of shade. You'll have all the hay and grain and cool water you want. Maybe you'll meet another good-lookin' Appaloosa. And the ocean. You've never seen the ocean, Fan. I'll bet you'd like swimming in it. I know I would. I think I'll buy me a bathing suit and we'll jump in there." He looked back again. Her eyes didn't open but she flicked her ears.

Hunger drove Jerry to open his last can of beans. Gagging at the taste, he forced himself to eat as he walked. The beans didn't need to be heated; he could hardly hold onto the hot tin can. At dusk he ate his last can of peaches and gulped down the sweet liquid. They tasted as good as the ice cream in Springerville, but the sweetness only added to his thirst.

They were out of food except for three slices of bread, their canteen was less than half full, and they had only a handful of grain left. Jerry had to face the truth. *If we don't come to Indio soon we're at the end of the line.* Jerry fed Fan the last of her

159

oats. He tore the three slices of bread into pieces and held them in cupped hands toward her. The bread disappeared and Fan nudged him for more.

Tears stung Jerry's eyes and ran down his face. The sight of Fan eating stale bread and wanting more hurt more than his own hunger. "Horses shouldn't have to eat dried-out bread, especially you. You shouldn't even be here in this God-forsaken place." Jerry rubbed Fan's muzzle; she nuzzled his hand, wanting food. He turned and started walking.

"You don't know anything about a bet, or Jimmy Wakely saying cowboyin' is dead. You have no idea that there's a Hollywood up ahead with cool water and plenty of food. You must think I've led you into hell and you're going to die." Afraid to falter, Jerry didn't turn around. He talked to the desert and hoped that the despair he felt didn't filter through his voice for Fan to hear. He kept his pace steady but refused to look back. It hurt too much to see what he had done to his horse.

Jerry couldn't stop; he couldn't comfort Fan. He could only put one foot in front of another and wonder *Could the compass be wrong? Did I somehow miscalculate? Maybe we're nowhere near Indio. God, what if we're walking in circles?* He thought about putting Fan out of her misery or letting her go but he could not bring himself to do either. An inner voice told him to not give up, that Fan would die without him and he without her. He looked all around and seeing no one decided the voice must be his own. Jerry Van Meter was saying not to give up.

Dark settled over the desert at the end of their third day. *If we don't find Indio this is it. We won't make it through another day. God, don't let Fan quit, don't let her lay down and give up. I won't leave her. If she stops it'll be the end of both of us.* With the truth came peace; it was comforting to know that he would not leave Fan, no matter what. After all they'd been through he would not leave her to die alone. He owed her that much – either Fan would walk out of this desert with him or he would stay with her until the end. Jerry's emotional mind told him their situation was hopeless; his rational mind told him he'd set the right compass course and Indio had to be somewhere close.

The quarter moon cast a pale light over the sand. Jerry walked, glancing up at millions of stars, then scanning the landscape for lights, any sign of a city. They *had* to have come thirty miles; he should be able to see it. Imperceptibly the desert floor changed but it took several minutes for it to register that something was different. Jerry's heart started pounding. His legs trembled and his lungs burned. *What's happening? Am I dying?*

It suddenly dawned on Jerry that the ground was no longer flat; he was walking uphill. He looked back. Fan hadn't changed her pace. The climb seemed endless; he had no idea how long it took. When finally the desert leveled out, Jerry found himself standing on a knoll, and, for the first time since leaving the Colorado River, he could see distance. Off to his right he saw the silhouette of low mountains and more mountains outlined against the sky to the south. And instead of only desert, only sky, Jerry saw a beautiful sight. A cluster of lights twinkled in the distance, a far-off Mecca sparkling with the promise of life.

"That has to be Indio, Fan. If we can see it we can make it. Come on, girl, let's get out of this desert."

# 27

## Is That Real Shade or a Mirage?

*Indio Press Enterprise*, June 15, 1946 // Indio Remains Hub of Coachella Valley Agricultural Industry // ⅜ Sq Mile Downtown Garners Indio Dubious Distinction as Smallest City in Country // Philippine Independence Inaugural Set for July 4 in Manila

Jerry wasn't sure whether the buildings in front of him were a product of his sun-baked delirium or real barns and stables with shade so deep his sunburned eyes couldn't penetrate it. The sun had been up for an hour when he led Fan under the Riverside County Fairgrounds sign and into the building it marked. When his eyes adjusted he could see horses peeking at them from out of their stalls. To make sure it wasn't a dream, he touched the nearest wall and took a deep breath. The wood felt rough to the touch, and the barn smells were wonderfully familiar. Only then did Jerry believe they had made it. A cowboy materialized out of the shade and walked toward them, his look of surprise quickly changing to shock and alarm. "My God, man, did I see right? Did you just walk in off the desert?"

Jerry nodded and looked around, not sure what to do first, wanting to savor, if only for a moment, their victory over the desert. Shade. Wonderful, blessed shade. His eyes came to rest on the fancy-dressed cowboy still staring at them. Jerry's look must have spurred him to action, for the cowboy turned on his heel and ran, immediately returning with a bucket of water. Jerry placed it under Fan's muzzle and she sucked up half of the water in a single drink. He splashed water over her face and let her drink the rest. "Tastes good, huh?" he whispered. His voice sounded strange, not like his own. It hurt to talk.

His throat felt like dried jerky; all the water in the world could not make it moist again.

The cowboy sprinted off with the empty bucket and came back in an instant with it full again. This time, Jerry plunged both hands in and splashed water over his face and head and then drank from his cupped hands. Cool and sweet, the water tasted like it had come right out of the well at the Bar R. Fan nudged forward, wanting more. The cowboy held the bucket for her and she drank the rest of the water in one long, slow drink.

"Come on," the cowboy said. "You don't need to be standing here. Both of you need help and fast." Jerry followed silently. Leading them away from the desert entrance to an empty stall in the middle of the large barn, the cowboy opened the stall gate. "Let me get her saddle off for you. You don't look like you have the strength to lift it."

Jerry shook his head. "I'll do it," he whispered.

"Well, what can I do? I know something half-dead when I see it."

"My horse needs food, Timothy hay if they have it. And rolled oats. Here, I'll get the m – " Jerry started to reach in his pocket.

The cowboy took off in a run. "Don't worry about it," he shouted over his shoulder. "Be right back."

Fan stood still as Jerry removed her bridle. He unbuckled the cinch and tried to lift the saddle. It wouldn't budge and it felt ten times heavier than usual. With trembling arms, he tried again; this time the saddle came off. Jerry hoisted it up onto the top rail of the stall. The saddle blanket came off with it and fell to the floor. Jerry glanced down at the blanket and saw the hide at the same time that the smell of raw, putrid flesh hit him. Like a hot furnace blast the stench of foul, decaying tissue exploded in his nostrils, filling the stall. Jerry gagged and gasped for air.

He could only stare dumbfounded at his horse. Great patches of skin had come off Fan's back and were still attached to the steamy saddle blanket. Too stunned to react, Jerry blinked unbelieving and looked again. It was true. Huge raw, bloody sores invaded by pus covered Fan's back. Her skin had literally cooked from the moisture and heat under her saddle.

Jerry's head swam. He went down on his knees, no longer able to stand, unable to speak. Shock, fatigue, and guilt overtook him, stomping him in the gut as they raced though his exhausted system to wreak havoc on his heart. Tears ran down his cheeks and Jerry covered his face with his hands, silently rocking back and forth on his knees. *I can't take anymore. This is too much. I am killing my horse.*

The squeak of an approaching wheelbarrow echoed through the barn. *The guy with the hay.* Jerry struggled to his feet and wiped his face with his sleeve. Parking the wheelbarrow in front of Fan's stall the cowboy looked over the gate. Eyes wide, he let out a low whistle. "My God, look at that," he whispered.

Jerry said nothing. There was nothing he could say.

The cowboy glanced at him, his eyes betraying instant awareness. "Hey, come on, it'll be okay. I could fetch a vet, but I think if we clean the sores and put some Bag Balm on them she'll get well on her own. What do you think?"

Jerry shook his head. "I don't know . . . sounds like the right thing. I need to get the pus off, but I don't have any disinfectant and I'm out of Bag Balm. I don't know what to – "

"You could use some help, partner. The name's Kevin Lamb, from Idaho." He reached through the stall gate and touched Fan's muzzle. "You could use some help, too."

Jerry nodded. "We must look pretty pitiful. Guess we both could."

Kevin picked up the bucket of water that was balanced on top of the hay bale and handed it over the rail. "I'll be back as quick as I can with some disinfectant, a can of Bag Balm, everything we need to take care of your horse. You quit worrying and drink some more water. We'll have your mare tended to in no time."

164

Jerry took a long drink and gave Fan the rest; she emptied the bucket. "Fan, what have I done to you? We made it, but at what price?"

Her whole demeanor shouted defeat: head drooped as low as it would go, tail hanging limp, not making any effort to swish away the flies that buzzed around her. Jerry leaned against the wall and closed his eyes against the painful sight. He was still leaning against it twenty minutes later, sound asleep and empty bucket in hand, when Kevin came back.

"Jerry, wake up. Let's take care of your horse, then you can get cleaned up and you both can sleep."

Jerry opened his eyes. It took a moment for him to realize they weren't in the desert anymore. Exhaustion, hunger, and dehydration had conquered him like it had his horse. He blinked, and his eyes focused slowly. His body didn't want to move. All defenses were down, but Fan needed immediate attention.

Kevin had changed from his fancy western duds into worn jeans and shirt and scuffed boots that looked as shabby as Jerry's. He had a shock of short blond hair and blue eyes that emanated sparks of kindness and compassion when he looked at Fan and a fellow cowboy. He led the way to the washing area, turned on the hose, and handed it to Jerry.

Jerry let the cool water flow over Fan and they both began cleaning her. They worked on both sides, first soaping off the dirt and dry crusted sweat. It pained Jerry to look at her back and it hurt even more to gaze upon a horse so totally spent. She looked half dead. Fan reached for the stream of water and Jerry held it steady so she could drink.

"Got your favorite hay waiting for you and some oats," he said softly. "You're in the shade. There's plenty of water. You can sleep and rest as long as you need. I want you to feel good again like you used to." Jerry choked back tears. His heart was breaking; he could hear it in his voice.

To Jerry's surprise, Kevin was doing his own reassuring. "Fan, huh? Is that your name, pretty lady? You don't look so pretty right now, but you will when we get you all fixed up." He bent down and massaged her legs with soapy rags. "How's that feel? She's going to be fine, Jerry. Her legs are tired but they don't seem injured. This is one strong horse. She'll come back." Kevin seemed to be reading Jerry's mind.

"You think? I hope so. Fan's such a great horse. I'd hate to think I . . ." Jerry looked away and gritted his teeth.

After they had scrubbed her, Jerry rinsed away the sweat and soap. The bath helped. Fan did none of her usual stretching or shaking, but she kept seeking the stream of water and drinking. He could feel her skin cool as they began to rub her down.

"She's a strong horse, but I'm surprised she could carry your weight across the desert," Kevin said as he knelt to dry her flank.

"I never rode her. My mistake was not taking her saddle off from the time we left the Colorado River. We never stopped for more than ten or fifteen minutes at a time. I was afraid if we did I'd fall asleep and never wake up." Jerry shuddered, picturing the pile of bleached bones.

Kevin straightened up and stared at him across Fan's withers. "You mean to tell me you walked across the Mojave Desert? That's a hundred miles!"

Jerry nodded. "I know." He kept trying to tell himself that Fan's injuries were temporary, unfortunate side effects of the trip, but he knew better. What he had put her through could have permanent consequences. *What if she couldn't come back?* Jerry could not erase the picture of her plodding along behind him through what could only be described as hell on earth or forget the moment he thought about putting her out of her misery.

Kevin interrupted his gruesome thoughts. "I ride the rodeo circuit all over the west, calf roping. I've seen horses with sores under their saddles lots of times. They get bunged up just like cowboys. You just have to know what to do and keep doing it," he said.

166

Fan flinched when Jerry and Kevin cleaned the pus from her wounds. They patted each raw spot with clean cloths soaked in hydrogen peroxide. Kevin noted Jerry's stricken look. "Her raw skin's a little tender, Jerry, but the peroxide doesn't hurt. I think this is hurting you more than Fan."

It didn't take long with the two of them working to clean and doctor the sores. Kevin disposed of the pus-covered rags and they applied Bag Balm with more clean cloths. Halfway through the application, Fan fell asleep.

"I think it's important to keep flies off those sores," Kevin said. "I've got a rotating fan I carry with me. That would move the air across her back and help the sores scab quicker. Keep her more comfortable, too. What do you say?"

"Can you sleep in this heat without it?"

Kevin patted Fan's withers. "I'm a softy when it comes to horses, and this one is special. I wish I didn't have to be in Los Angeles tomorrow, but you're welcome to use the fan until I leave."

Jerry walked with Fan back to the stall. Kevin ran ahead. By the time Fan and Jerry arrived he had spread a thick layer of fresh straw over the floor. He'd piled her favorite kind of hay in the corner and filled a low round pan with rolled oats. Kevin held up a handful of hay. "Here, Fan, after what you've been through, this is the equine equivalent of a chocolate fudge sundae. Eat up, girl."

The stall still smelled of putrid flesh. Fan's saddle blanket that had been thrown over the railing reeked of it. Kevin told Jerry to get his things together for a shower and disappeared with the blanket. Jerry leaned against the wall, content to see Fan cleaned up and eating. Kevin came back a few minutes later without the blanket. "I cleaned and hosed it off real good, used a bar of lye on it. It's hanging out back in the sun. That ought to disinfect the heck out of it. I'll be back in a second. I'm going to get the fan from my room. I'll bring you a clean towel while I'm at it."

167

He directed Jerry to the small, board-enclosed shower next to the horse washing area. Jerry wrapped himself in his dirty towel and walked with tender feet. The tiny stall had cold water only, but it couldn't have felt any better out of gold faucets at the Ritz Hotel. Jerry stood under the spray and was shaving his face and neck by feel when Kevin returned with a clean towel and the fan. "This feels so good I hate to get out, but I need food." He brushed his teeth and put on a clean shirt and jeans. Clothes that weren't stiff with sweat felt almost as good as the shower. His mouth tasted fresh like toothpaste and Jerry's hair smelled of pine-scented soap. But his feet could not be that easily relieved. The bottoms felt like they had been fried on a griddle. Refusing to look, he gritted his teeth, then applied some Bag Balm and willed them to get better.

By the time Fan had drunk her fill, all-told she had consumed seven or eight gallons of water. She ate half of the oats and a little of the hay and then abruptly stopped. She lowered herself onto the straw and lay flat out, the picture of a horse beyond exhaustion. Tears stung Jerry's eyes.

Kevin gave him a "don't worry, she's going to be okay" look. He secured the oscillating fan to the top rail, faced it down toward Fan's back and then turned it on. The fan hummed and clicked as it rotated from side to side, ruffling the loose straw around the sleeping mare. She did not move. Except for her side rising and lowering in rhythm with each breath, Fan looked dead.

"You being a cowboy, I don't mind telling you how much it hurts to see her this way," Jerry said quietly, trying to keep the catch out of his voice. "Thanks for all your help. As beat as I am, that would have been tough to do by myself."

Kevin spoke softly, his eyes on Fan. "You're welcome, Jerry. More than welcome. That's one special horse. She's got heart. That's why I know she'll come back. The important thing is she's taken care of, watered and fed and sound asleep – the best thing for her and exactly what *you* need. You must be starving. Let me scrub up and change my clothes. We can't do anything more for Fan now. Let's go get a bite of breakfast. I'm dying to hear the story that goes with you staggering in off the desert."

# 28

## The Blue-Plate Special

*Indio Press Enterprise*, June 15, 1946 // Indio Population Projected 112,000 by Year 2,000 // Pitchers Feller, Newhouser & Chandler Tilt Odds to American League in Upcoming All-Star Clash // Vietnam Uprising Sparks War with France

Indio had a tiny downtown no more than a half-mile long. Jerry followed Kevin into the coffee shop located in the New Traveler's Hotel and Café. The ten a.m. sun glistened off deserted sidewalks and created shimmering waves of heat in the still morning air. Covered roofs extended out over the sidewalks in front of some of the buildings. Good idea, Jerry thought, as he took a last look before entering the cafe. Indio seemed like a nice little town but nothing like Springerville. But then at forty degrees hotter, Jerry found it hard to think at all. The waitress led them to a booth directly under a ceiling fan and placed two glasses of water on the table. At the first smell of food, Jerry's hunger awoke. "I need something more than breakfast. Got any suggestions?" He put the water glass to his lips. "Ouch. These sores hurt."

"The blue-plate special is chicken fried steak and homemade biscuits. All I have to do is mash the potatoes. Would you like that?" the waitress asked.

"The blue-plate special sounds good," Jerry said. Kevin ordered the same. A few minutes later, when he eyed the sizzling piece of chicken fried steak and mountain of mashed potatoes and cream gravy on the plate in front of him, Jerry realized the depths of his hunger. "These sores are going to make it tough to eat." He made a concentrated effort to eat slowly. When he had finally pushed away the plate, not a morsel remained.

Kevin must have said "I'll be damned" twenty times during their meal. Jerry told him all about the bet, Jimmy Wakely, his grandfather and Frank, right down to the border guard warning him not to sneak across. "I did anyway, fifteen miles north of Ehrenberg. Have you heard anything about this interdiction?"

"No, not a word. But I just came down from the San Joaquin Valley so I haven't been anywhere near the border. Nobody's been asking questions around the fairgrounds though. Maybe they're just clamping down on it between here and the state line."

Jerry shook his head. "If it hadn't been for the interdiction we wouldn't have come across the desert in the first place. Didn't want to run into the law. I'd hate to think Fan and me went through that ordeal for nothing."

Kevin pushed away his empty plate. "Well, I'm sure there is one, no reason for the guard to lie. If they wouldn't let me across after coming all that way, I'd have done the same thing."

The friendly waitress came by to check and, finding clean plates, told them they had earned a free dessert. She brought out two dishes of vanilla pudding over sliced bananas on a base of vanilla wafers, and Jerry had his first cup of coffee in over a week. Both cowboys finished off their dessert and Jerry paid for their meals with a five dollar bill.

"You the cook?" he asked. The waitress nodded hesitantly as she gave him his change. "You have to be from Oklahoma. That dessert and the cream gravy could have come right out of my mother's kitchen in Guthrie. And I loved those Okie biscuits."

She beamed. "I *am* from Oklahoma. Born in Ardmore."

"Well, you're one fine cook," Jerry said. "A great meal."

Kevin thanked Jerry for lunch as they walked back along Highway 111 to the fairgrounds at the corner of Oasis and Arabia streets. They stopped beside his truck and horse trailer parked in the shade of the largest building. "I'm leaving early tomorrow, calf roping in the Gene Autry Rodeo in L.A. I could drive you right to Hollywood. Got an extra stall." He patted his dusty trailer. "Nobody would have to know."

"I would know." Jerry couldn't help but notice the tall, skinny palm trees to the west of the fairgrounds. He hadn't seen them when he stumbled in off the desert. Jerry nodded toward the trees with a questioning look at Kevin.

Kevin turned around. "Oh, those things are date palms." He turned back to Jerry. "Somehow I knew you wouldn't take me up on my offer. By the way, where are you going when you get to Hollywood?"

"Haven't figured that out yet. I want to meet up with Jimmy Wakely if he's at his ranch. I'm not sure he's even in Hollywood. He might be away on a singing tour. Exactly what are dates?"

Kevin led the way back into the barn; Jerry followed. "They're sort of like a prune, only sweeter and not as wrinkled. You mean to tell me you started out for Hollywood and don't have a place to stay when you get there?" Kevin had an incredulous look on his face.

They approached Fan's stall and both looked over the rail. She hadn't moved. "That's about the size of it," Jerry said quietly. "Think I'll try me some of those dates. I've never even heard of them."

Kevin laughed and shook his head, his eyebrows raised in disbelief. "You Oklahoma cowboys are tough, but crazy. One of my best friends lives in Hollywood. Go to his place. He'll put you up. His name is Pete Wilson, head stuntman for Republic Pictures. Pete's got twenty acres in North Hollywood, trains his trick horses there. We used to ride rodeos together. Now he only rides if there's one near his home. I never had the brains to get out."

"Exactly what does he do?"

172

"He takes the fall for the star, say, John Wayne. He did it for Hoot Gibson and Hopalong Cassidy when they were Republic stars. When a horse supposedly gets shot out from under the star and sends him ass over tea kettle you can bet it isn't Jimmy Wakely or Roy Rogers rolling through the dust . . . or their fancy horse either. If it's a Republic movie, it's Pete and one of his horses. He's been doing it for fifteen years."

"I could have used a stuntman on this trip."

"Hell, Oklahoma, you could *be* a stuntman. You've sure got the experience." Kevin wrote down Pete Wilson's address and a brief note to him and then gave Jerry general directions. "Sorry my directions aren't more exact, but not all the streets around his place have names. Anyway, give this to Pete and I'll stop by before I head out of Los Angeles. I wish you'd come with me, make it easy on yourself and that horse of yours. Fan's going to get better, but it's another hundred and fifty miles to Hollywood and still plenty hot."

"I know. Sounds tempting, but I can't. I've come too far to cheat. I'm not going to ride her for a while yet. I've got an idea to fix the blanket so nothing touches her back."

"Well, I wish you and Fan the best of luck. You're a helluva cowboy, Oklahoma," Kevin said. They shook hands.

"Thanks again for all the help. You ain't bad yourself, Idaho. I hope we meet again. Don't forget to take your fan."

"I'll get it in the morning after I load up my horses. By the time you wake up, I'll be halfway there." They spoke quietly, watching Fan as they talked. The cowboy from Idaho with the kind blue eyes gave a silent wave and disappeared.

It was almost noon when Jerry finally spread his bedroll against the wall in Fan's stall and took off his boots. His body ached with an all-encompassing weariness, and sleep beckoned with a power he could no longer fight. Feeling himself losing consciousness Jerry lay down, aware only of the fan's rhythmic swooshing noise and air moving across him. His skin wasn't on fire; he wasn't dirty and hungry anymore. And most important he and Fan were alive; they still had a chance. He glanced briefly at his sleeping horse, closed his eyes and slept. It had been eighty-two hours since he had awakened at two a.m. at the Colorado River, unable to sleep because of pesky insects and the daunting journey ahead.

Jerry accomplished a lot in the two days he spent in Indio. He fashioned Fan's clean saddle blanket into a protective cover that allowed nothing to touch her healing skin. Folding the blanket into several thicknesses, he cut holes in it the exact size of her sores. The thick blanket layers now rested on healthy skin and left an air space over the scabbed-over sores where neither blanket nor saddle could touch.

He trimmed her hooves and put new rock shoes on. Like the worn out ones he replaced, they were made of thick iron and rimmed with a one inch lip to make them last longer. They were evidently not designed to be worn crossing the Mojave Desert because Jerry could bend her old rock shoes with his fingers; they were paper thin.

He groomed Fan and fed her sweet, ripe apples for treats. He replenished his food supplies – no beans on the list. He hoped he would never have to eat them again. Jerry bought a bag of dates and ate them like candy. He wrote a letter to his parents and brothers, also one to Rolla and Frank. When he thought about trying to tell them about crossing the desert, Jerry decided no words could describe the experience, so he just wrote that he didn't much care for it.

And he slept. Automatically, the moment he lay down on his bedroll he fell asleep. Fan did the same – on her feet after the first day. Except for a twenty-minute walk through the shady complex of open barns twice a day to keep her limber, Fan spent her time in Indio either eating, drinking, or sleeping. Jerry watched her come back to life like a wilted flower after it has been watered.

The last evening in the tiny desert city brought a treat. A freak Pacific storm roared up through the Gulf of California, bringing with it cooler air, lightning, thunder, and rain. The storm lingered for the whole evening before it blew out over the desert. The arrival of rain brought out the Indio residents Jerry had yet to see, enjoying "the gift," as they called it.

He left Indio at dawn the following morning by the same means he had arrived – on foot and leading his horse. It was June 17, day forty-five, and they had one hundred forty miles to go to reach Hollywood. "Fan, we're gonna be in Hollywood by day fifty, come hell or high water. We've been through both and neither one has stopped us."

# 29

## The Place That God Forgot

*California Highway Patrolman Magazine*, June, 1946 // California Celebrates 50-Year Anniversary of First Motor Car // Freight Shipments, Passenger Travel to Europe, South America Expected to Increase Air Travel by 50% // 40M Aircraft, Auto, and Ordnance Parts Built in 1,249 Days of War

A leaner, more determined Jerry Van Meter walked out of Indio before daylight on June 17, 1946. He began the last leg of his journey feeling he could look Rolla and Frank in the eye now, man to man, and not have to hang his head about anything.

Leading Fan west alongside railroad tracks, he passed rows of long tin packing sheds already humming with activity. They went through what, in the dark, looked like a shantytown – tiny shacks with people sleeping outside, others beginning to stir. Campfires glowed in front of the shacks. Women moved about, bending low over their fires, tending pots that filled the rain-freshened air with pungent smells. It reminded Jerry of Cibecue only there was no Indian rodeo and these fires weren't to feed Apache onlookers in a festive mood. They were to feed hundreds of Mexican workers helping to produce and harvest the agricultural riches of the Coachella Valley. Jerry and Fan passed fields of row crops that were unidentifiable in the dark and acres of tall date palms, their thin trunks and pom-pom tops poking fifty and sixty feet into the sky. He wondered how dates were harvested.

Despite what he'd heard from Kevin, Jerry didn't want to chance running into a patrolman or anyone who might know about the interdiction and summon the authorities. The north side of Highway 10 belonged to the federal government. He had asked the waitress at the coffee shop about it. No development and no people, it would be a mile or two out of the way but worth it. They crossed the darkened highway and walked north and west. When he could no longer see lights or hear cars, Jerry corrected their course to due west.

Again they were in the wide-open desert, though it looked different than the landscape they had covered in the dark when approaching Indio. Not flat and endless, but the desert nonetheless – bright moon glistening off light sand, sparse vegetation specialized to survive in arid climates. Jerry noticed a new shape he hadn't seen before. Tall silhouettes that looked like trees but with prickly limbs like the cactus. He busied himself spotting shadowy shapes and weaving around and between them to avoid rattlesnakes.

The desert's familiarity was comforting. He had conquered it before; he could do so again. Still, it brought an element of fear. The sand, the eerie shapes, and the heat combined to re-create the feeling in Jerry's gut. The same feeling he'd had just before spotting Indio's distant lights when he realized he and Fan would not last another day. It was a memory too fresh to ignore, and Jerry shook himself then looked back at Fan to dispel the morbid thoughts. Her head was up; she looked alert. "How you doing back there?" Her ears flicked back and forth, and she nickered softly. "Well, I'll be damned, you actually answered." Jerry couldn't call Fan's step lively, but it was certainly more energetic than it had been across the Mojave.

Jerry felt the same way. His step betrayed a new-found confidence. No longer an unknown, he knew the desert for what it was: one more enemy in a long line of enemies, differing only from a raging river or a Rocky Mountain snowstorm, or from men wanting to kill him in that this enemy used unforgiving, never-ending heat.

Jerry's original plan to follow Highway 10 across the desert had been a good one, well thought out but with one very important hitch. An unforeseen law and an officious border guard had nearly cost them their lives. While relating the story to Kevin, it occurred to Jerry that his fear of Fan being impounded, his fatigue, and the endless heat had combined to influence his thinking. Leaving the safety of the highway had been a crucial decision – almost fatal. He would not make the same mistake twice. Jerry intended to stay out of the law's reach, but this time within reasonable limits.

The sun came up, dispelling the freshness of the previous night's storm and replacing it with blinding glare and blistering heat. The new shapes turned out to be Joshua trees, tall thorny-branched brothers of the yucca plant. They cast meager but welcome shade. Still part of the Mojave, this desert looked different, a series of low, rolling hills. When he looked out towards the north, the desert's surface reminded him of the gently rolling hills of Oklahoma, only covered with sand instead of crops. No ordinary desert, this one had a story.

According to the waitress at the New Traveler's Hotel coffee shop, this desert had been home to one of America's biggest war heroes. During last night's dinner she had told the story in segments on her intermittent stops at his table. General George Patton and his wife, Beatrice, had been Indio residents for a brief time during the war. Young George had grown up in southern California and later as a general felt that the Mojave was not just similar to the North African desert, it was worse. Because of his knowledge of the Mojave, the War Department picked him to establish and command a Desert Training Center (DTC) in the early months of 1942. Overnight the army flooded the area with soldiers and trucks and equipment. Airplanes flew in and out with important Washington brass on board. Armored tanks and flat-tracks could be seen being unloaded off railcars near Desert Center. Suddenly the two thousand residents of Indio and the rest of Coachella Valley found themselves smack in the middle of the war.

For the few days before he moved his base camp twenty

miles east of Indio, General Patton and his staff had used the New Traveler's Hotel as their headquarters. The waitress said the general's voice could be heard "from one end of town to the other." That reminded Jerry of Rolla and Frank's stories about Charlie Goodnight's blistering language and bellowing voice.

Jerry chuckled aloud when he realized he and Fan had walked through the same desert General Patton used to train troops and tank commandos in survival and desert warfare. The waitress had said that the first troops to arrive at the DTC had called it "the place that God forgot." Jerry knew exactly what they meant. "Hey, Fan. Since we beat this desert, think we can survive most anything?" Jerry looked back at Fan, confident that no greater truth could be said. All told, over two million DTC troops and tank commanders had survived training exercises in this ten thousand square miles of desert with General Patton. The same personnel and equipment of the Second Corps helped him defeat the Germans in the North African deserts and later in Sicily.

Jerry walked for three hours and then stopped for a thirty-minute rest, this time removing Fan's saddle and turning it on its side in the shade. The warm air dried the sweat on her back and reduced the moisture that accumulated in the saddle blanket. A time-consuming process, but it worked; the scabs remained intact. It also ate up precious ticks of the clock.

Remembering how Fan had responded to his and Kevin's voice, Jerry sang as he walked, all the good cowboy songs he could recall. When he ran out of songs, Jerry talked. "You're helping Grandpa win a bet for cowboys everywhere, prove horses are as tough today as they ever were. You're tougher than any horse I ever heard of, Fan." He talked about the pretty sights they had seen and the people they had met. He figured that Fan might not know *what* he said, but she would know by the tone of his voice that this time it held no despair.

The heat was as unmerciful, and the sun equally blinding,

but this time Jerry had no trouble with concentration. He harbored no thought of letting Fan go or that they might not make it. The difference had little to do with occasional shade or proximity to a highway. The desert that had threatened him from the beginning was no longer a great unknown. Jerry knew its limits and now he knew his own.

At four P.M. he adjusted the angle of his path to a more southerly direction, and half an hour later the highway came back into view. As they got closer, Jerry scanned the stretch of asphalt in both directions for black and white Packards but saw none. He led Fan across the highway, back over the railroad tracks, and headed into the eastern outskirts of Palm Springs.

# 30

## The Long Arm of the Law

*The Desert Sun*, June 18, 1946 // Meat Shortage? Lots of Beef But It's All on the Hoof // Four Lanes for Palm Canyon Dr. – Lights Will Replace Stop Signs // Directors Edgar Bergen, Leonard Firestone Form Corporation to Develop Former DTC Tank Repair Facility

"We could have bummed a ride on the train in Indio and saved ourselves walking all day and some sore, hot feet. You ever been on a train, Fan?" Jerry looked back, expecting to see a lethargic horse plodding along. Instead she had speeded up, and there was a new determination in her step. Ten minutes later he found out why. A river running along the edge of a huge orange grove lay directly in their path.

Fan walked down the bank into the water and immediately started to drink. She kept one eye and ear trained on Jerry, the other scanning the orchard to her right. The river looked to be more of a canal, but the water ran slowly and was deep enough to reach the underside of Fan's belly. Jerry sat on the weed-covered bank, eyeing the orange orchard while she drank. He could hardly wait to walk into its inviting shade.

Looking toward the west, he saw that the orchard continued; the mass of green seemed to go on forever. At five o'clock, the hottest hour of the day, the sun's fiery rays shined directly into Jerry's weary eyes, snaking underneath his hat brim and rendering his Stetson useless. He considered removing his boots and joining Fan, then he noticed her looking around like she wanted to lie down in the water. Jerry didn't have time to remove his boots before reacting. He jumped in and grabbed an apple from his saddlebag. Only then did Fan willingly follow him out of the canal and into the deep shade of the orange grove.

"You would have gotten everything wet." Jerry's jeans were soaked up to his pockets, and with each step his boots squished water over the tops. "How can I get upset with you? At least my legs are cool."

Jerry hurriedly switched Fan from bridle to halter and tethered her to a tree; she wanted the apple he'd promised. Her expectant happy-face expression greeted his outstretched hand full of apple slices. "You and your treats. I wish I had one of those strawberry cones about now." He removed her saddle, pleased to see that the scabs had remained intact with no sign of pus.

The orchard had recently been irrigated. Wide furrows ran down the center of each row; they were muddy at the bottom, with damp earth on the higher ground directly under the trees. Jerry walked to the edge of the orchard opposite from where they had entered. A two-lane road divided it, then trees continued on the other side and in both directions. He watched as Mexican workers exited the orchard across the road and loaded their ladders into pickup trucks. Jerry quickly stepped back into the trees.

A concrete standpipe, the source of the irrigation water, stood at the end of the row. Jerry reached down inside the pipe and turned on the valve. The standpipe immediately began to fill and water bubbled up and over the sides. He washed his face and drank from his cupped hands then walked back to Fan. "I know where you can get a drink of water later." Jerry had never been in an orange orchard before. *Mature trees, judging by the size of their trunks and their height,* he thought. And despite the heat and blinding sun a few hundred yards away, deep in the orchard it felt cool. The air smelled sweet, and water bubbled up out of the ground on demand.

Jerry reasoned that if the Mojave represented hell on earth, this had to be heaven. Fan ate a bigger-than-usual portion of oats. Jerry ate a peanut butter sandwich, food with no other purpose than to keep him alive.

He stretched out on his bedroll under a tree, and the feeling of weariness came again. But more than weariness or simple fatigue, it was exhaustion, an acceptance that his body could go no farther, that it had no more to give. It wasn't pain, but heavy limbs and heavy eyes, a rapturous calm that started at his feet and moved upward through his body to the end of his fingers laced loosely across his chest. Jerry closed his eyes and let himself be enveloped by the coolness, the fragrance, the absence of the blinding sun.

"I know you're every bit this tired, Fan. Better lay down while you got a shady soft spot to do it," he called to her sleepily. From the sound of her steady breathing, Fan was already asleep.

In the fog of deep sleep, Jerry felt something touch the bottom of his feet. The touch was not enough to rouse him from his trance-like state, but when it came again a little harder and with a steady tap, tap, tap, his eyes flew open. He found himself looking straight into the blinding beam of a flashlight. "What the h – ?" He tried to sit up, but pressure on his chest pushed him back to the ground. For a frightening moment Jerry could not remember where they were.

"Now what do we have here? A vagrant?" The owner of the voice must have already spotted Fan. "I've never seen a vagrant with a horse." The beam moved off Jerry's face. "Sit up, mister, nice and slow."

Jerry sat up, blinking and trying to focus. From his vantage point he could only see the sharp crease of a pant leg, about knee level. Jerry's eyes followed the crease down to the top of a shiny black shoe. *Oh my God, the highway patrol.* His heart hammered as he tried to sit up. "I'm not a vagrant." His mind raced, sick with dread. "Is it okay if I stand up?"

"Are you carrying a weapon?" came the voice from above him.

"Yes sir, holster's hanging on a limb above my saddle."

"Go ahead, stand up, but no sudden moves please," the patrolman said with pure authority.

Once upright and on his feet, Jerry's tired muscles told him he hadn't been asleep very long. He raised his hands, squinting against the beam. The officer moved the light away from his face and Jerry stood staring directly into the eyes of a California highway patrolman. He looked to be about his dad's age. Black hair showed from under a soft-billed cap, and his curious eyes did not match the sternness in his voice. He held a nightstick in his right hand.

In the dim light Jerry saw that he was dressed exactly like the officers at the border: hip-length jacket, a wide belt lined with bullets, and a holster with a revolver. He had a seven point badge pinned on the left side of his jacket, but Jerry couldn't make out the writing in the darkness.

"I can explain what I'm doing here. I look bad, but I'm not a bum." *God, I hope he doesn't know about the interdiction.*

"Let's have a look at that weapon." The officer lifted the six-shooter from Jerry's holster. "Hmmh, notches." Spinning the cylinder, he methodically ejected each bullet into his hand and dropped them into his coat pocket. "Got any identification?" He returned the empty Colt to the holster.

"Yes, sir." Jerry lowered his right hand and reached into his hip pocket. No wallet. Fear turned to panic before he remembered he'd put his wallet in the waterproof tin in his saddlebags. "Would you like me to get it?" *I don't have a choice, I'm going to have to tell him the truth.*

"Absolutely."

Fan had awakened, frightened by the strange voice and light. Alert, she tossed her head and whinnied. "It's okay, girl." Jerry patted her neck then knelt down to look through his saddlebags. "Look, officer, me and my mare have come over a thousand miles. I'm not up to anything bad. I can prove who I am. My name's Jerry Van Meter from Oklahoma. We're on our way to Hollywood."

184

"Where in Oklahoma?" The voice sounded a little friendlier.

"Guthrie, it's just north of Oklahoma City."

"I know where Guthrie is. We don't get many gun-toting cowboys around here. When somebody sees one camping out on private property, they get a little nervous. Let's see that ID."

The officer shined the flashlight beam over Jerry's shoulder as Jerry went through the tin box that held his papers. The calendar lay on top; he held it up for the officer. "See? I've marked off every day we've been on the road." He kept digging until he found his wallet on the bottom of the tin. "I keep my wallet in here. We've had to cross a couple of rivers." Jerry pulled out his Oklahoma driver's license and naval identification card and handed them to the officer.

"You can stand up and tend to your horse. I must be making it nervous." Jerry got to his feet and put his hand on Fan's withers, mouthing a silent prayer that the interdiction had been lifted, or if it hadn't, that this patrolman didn't know of it.

"Navy, huh?" the officer said. He read softly to himself from each card. "Okay, Jerry Van Meter from Guthrie, Oklahoma, what are you doing packing a Colt with notches in the handle and sleeping on private property in Palm Springs, California?"

"Where I live and in my business it's common to wear a holster and pistol."

"What is your business?"

"I'm a cowboy, foreman on my granddad's ranch near Enid, Oklahoma. We all wear them. The reason I'm in Palm Springs has to do with a bet my grandfather made with a friend of his, a movie star named Jimmy Wakely."

The officer relaxed his stance. He slipped the leather loop of his nightstick over a tree limb. "Any self-respecting western fan, which I happen to be, knows who Jimmy Wakely is. Okay,

185

now you've got my attention. Explain." His voice sounded completely friendly now.

Jerry went through the story again, emphasizing the long-standing friendship between Jimmy Wakely and his grand-father. When he finished with the part about his walking across the Mojave, the officer gave a low whistle. "That's the damnedest story I ever heard." He looked at Jerry with a mixture of admiration and incredulity. "So you rode *this* horse," he pointed to Fan, "all the way from Guthrie to the Colorado River. But why did you walk the rest of the way?" He handed Jerry back his identification.

"I was afraid that with the heat my horse wouldn't make it carrying my weight. She still got messed up. You should see her back." Jerry held his breath. *If he knows, this is when he'll hit me with the impound.*

The officer pointed the flashlight beam toward Fan and the scabs were easily visible. "I see what you mean." He shoved his cap back and rubbed his forehead. "That's too crazy to be a lie, no wonder you look so – "

Jerry exhaled with a chuckle. "I look good compared to what I looked like when we walked in off the desert. We call it trail dirty and saddle-weary. I haven't had a haircut since . . . Springerville, Arizona. I know I look awful but I'm so tired there's not much I can do about it."

"I can't imagine anybody walking across the Mojave Desert in this heat and surviving. But you. You look like you did it." He kept shaking his head in disbelief. "Where are you going once you get to Hollywood?"

Jerry handed the patrolman the note that Kevin had written to the Republic Pictures stuntman. "I'm from Oklahoma," the patrolman began. "My wife and I live over in Hemet now, lots of Okies there. The Hemet theater plays more westerns than anything else." He rattled off the names of Gene Autry and Roy Rogers movies that Jerry had never heard of. "My wife and I have probably seen every one of Jimmy Wakely's

186

pictures. I bet not more than a month ago we saw him in *Moon Over Montana*. He starred in that one." The officer cupped his chin; the flashlight in his other hand pointed straight down. "And I'm trying to remember, I'm sure I've heard the name Pistol Pete before."

"Pretty famous, actually. His real name is Frank Eaton. He's the one who put the notches in my Colt, long before I – "

"Wait a minute. Now I remember. Handlebar mustache, big ol' ten gallon hat, wears his hair in braids? Isn't he the Oklahoma State University mascot?"

"That's him. He'll be pleased you knew that."

"We still go back to Oklahoma City once in a while, lots of family there. Won't they get a kick when I tell them about running into you. It's been a pleasure meeting a real cowboy from my home state. I'll give you a little advice, though. I suggest you put the Colt in your saddlebag for the rest of your trip. Probably save you a lot of explaining."

"I'll do that."

The patrolman retrieved the bullets from his pocket and handed them to Jerry. "Sorry about waking you out of a sound sleep. Some fieldworkers called in that they'd seen a bum in here. Hope I didn't scare you half to death."

"That's okay. We're on private property. I understand. It's just that when we got to town we were so tired and hot this orchard practically called our names. My horse headed for the shade like she usually does water."

The patrolman chuckled. "Still can't imagine walking across the desert. Sounds to me like you've already had considerable good luck, but I'll wish more for you anyway. I hope you win the bet." He retrieved his nightstick.

"Thanks, I'm going to give it my best."

Jerry watched the flashlight beam disappear into the deepening darkness. When he could no longer see it, he took his first deep breath. "Close, Fan. I thought sure he'd run us in." Jerry lit a match and checked the time. "Nine o'clock. No

wonder I'm still tired. Think you can go back to sleep, Fan?"
He heard Fan's steady breathing. "Guess so." Jerry lay back
down on his bedroll.

The air felt cool. He could see tiny patches of stars through
the trees. *I'm hungry, I'll never get back to sleep.* With his last
waking thoughts of pie and ice cream, the fragrant air and
soft damp earth lulled Jerry back to sleep as soon as he closed
his eyes.

# 31

## Welcome to the Future

*The Desert Sun,* June 19, 1946 // War Assets Corp Delays Return of City Hospital Red Tape // Coloured Thief Offered 30-Day Sentence Reduction to Leave Town // Phenomenal Growth Predicted for Palm Springs

Jerry led Fan and walked west on Palm Canyon Drive the next morning, stopping at one of the restaurants flashing a bright neon sign "Open 24 Hours." He followed up a breakfast of ham and eggs with apple pie and ice cream for dessert. Palm Springs's main street bustled with new development. Buildings stood too far back from the road for him to see them, but what he could see bore no resemblance to the arid, desolate land east of Indio or the shantytown on the western outskirts of it. Palm-lined drives curved through and around spacious grounds. Expansive lawns surrounded elaborate fountains with waterfalls sparkling in the early morning sun.

He passed a sign pointing down a side street to Troy Roger's Mink and Manure Club, heralding it as Palm Springs's newest western nightspot. "Entertainment by Singer Patty Page, Direct from Hollywood." "I ought to stop in and see what California cowboys look like, Fan." He didn't have to go looking because Jerry encountered more horsemen along Palm Canyon Drive than he had at any time on the trip. They weren't cowboys, but members of riding clubs, and they stopped him and introduced themselves as being from this stable or that stable. One rider on a beautifully groomed Palomino asked Jerry outright why he led his horse. Was she injured, did they need help? He offered to accompany them to his riding club nearby. *Friendly people, these Californians.*

Palm Springs dazzled as much from growth as it did from sunny weather. There was new construction everywhere he looked. Jerry spotted a massive building in Thunderbird Ranch, a huge commercial site being developed. On closer inspection it turned out to be a high school slated for opening in September 1947. Farther on, another partially completed structure labeled "Future Home of Bullocks Department Store" occupied a sprawling site of unfinished commercial buildings. Signs pointed the way to Tom O'Donnell's Golf Course and Charlie Farrell's Racquet Club and Tennis Ranch. Jerry smiled. *I wonder exactly what they raise on a tennis ranch.* Flags and an elaborate sign marked the entrance to Tahquitz River Estates, a series of neat rows of houses laid out on wide streets, some of which were framed and others in varying states of completion. "Palm Springs's Best New Subdivision. Homes From $5,600."

Contrary to what he had read and heard, Jerry saw no evidence of a building material shortage. Workers scurried about carrying two-by-fours, bricks, and lengths of pipe; construction sounds filled the air. And it seemed every carpenter, plumber, and roofer drove a pickup truck – more pickups than Jerry had ever seen in one place. Here was progress, what Jimmy Wakely had witnessed and tried to warn Rolla and Frank about, "explosive growth, the reawakening of our country." Jimmy had called it right: "a postwar boom, the end of an era that would never return."

Not more than forty miles east, Jerry had left the desert that used to be. Now, in the midst of this city, everywhere he turned he saw a glimpse of what it was going to be. Phoenix had been the same. City boundaries stretching in all directions full of energy and promise, buildings springing up, roads being built, parking lots under construction where none had been before. Like crossing the Mojave, Jerry realized he could not capture this in a letter.

On the western outskirts of Banning, twenty miles west of

190

Palm Springs, Jerry decided to ride Fan again. The smaller scabs had come off and the larger ones remained intact. The blanket with holes cut to match her sores had worked as he'd planned. Now it would have to work with his weight on the saddle. Foot weary and exhausted, Jerry had walked more than one hundred thirty-five miles and he could walk no farther.

Wednesday, June 19, the forty-seventh day: if they did not arrive in Hollywood by Saturday they would lose the bet. Hollywood lay eighty miles north and west as the crow flies, and they could neither fly like a crow nor travel in a straight line. They had traffic and people to contend with; he would need time to find Pete Wilson's place. Jerry either had to ride or lose the bet. After the previous night's encounter with the highway patrol, the law no longer seemed to be a threat. Jerry rode alongside Highway 10, the quickest, most direct route into Los Angeles. Fan paid no attention to the cars whizzing by at fifty-five miles an hour, or the occasional honking horn. He had grown to love Fan, her nerve, her heart and endless loyalty, her acceptance of whatever life threw her way. It did not go unnoticed that those traits personified the man who had given her to him.

Up ahead Jerry spied three red and white Burma Shave signs. They called up instant memories of growing up during the Depression. With gas shortages and little money, the Van Meter family rarely took car trips. But when they did, Jimmy, Jerry, Billy, David, and Byron had an understanding: whoever spied the signs first got to read them aloud to the whole family.

Jerry guided Fan closer.

*Are your whiskers when you wake*
*Tougher than a two-bit steak?*
*Try Burma Shave.*

He rubbed his stubble-covered face and steered Fan back away from the road's edge. Reciting the rhyme under his breath he remembered drives years before with his parents and brothers to visit Rolla at the Bar R. Five boys crammed into the back seat of a 1931 Touring Studebaker and having to sit still for over an hour – it seemed like an eternity. The Studebaker barely came to a stop at the ranch, and they would burst out of the car like coiled springs and race to Grandpa's barns to play, yelling and laughing. Jerry's smile deepened at the thought. He rode past more citrus groves in Cherry Valley, Calimesa, and Redlands, each town a step farther from the desert.

At the western outskirts of San Bernardino, Jerry turned west and joined the last fifty miles of Route 66. Route 66 had wound through the hearts of cities, transporting people, commerce, ideas, and a fantasy about road travel like no other road had before. Young couples spent their honeymoons traveling the Mother Road. Starting in Chicago it raced westward and ended only when it ran out of real estate in Santa Monica at the ocean's edge.

Tired and dirty, Jerry welcomed the sight of it, like coming across an old friend. He thought back to the Oklahoma prairie and the night he camped beside the Mother Road, listening to the whine of diesel rigs, watching car lights race by in the fading light, wondering what adventures awaited him. Although separated for what seemed like a lifetime, here it was again, palm-lined and pointing the way, just like he'd dreamed about. Hollywood – the end of the journey, a covenant kept, a bet won.

On the north side of Route 66, an arch made from full debarked logs marked the entrance to the San Gabriel Riding Club. Jerry headed Fan under it and onto the club's spacious grounds. New roofs and buildings and immaculate grounds labeled it a new facility, its wooden fences painted crisp white. Straight rows of corrals, each one filled with groomed horses, formed avenues to the right of the driveway. Stableboys rushed back and forth carrying halters, saddles, and bridles.

192

Riders dressed in riding britches, tall slender boots, jackets, and small black hats stared with open mouths as Jerry and Fan rode in. Jerry noted that the stableboys dressed like cowboys – albeit clean-clothed, rested cowboys. He dismounted and led Fan past a bulletin board showing times for riding lessons and riding classes with names like "Show Techniques" and "Basic Horsemanship." He asked a stableboy if they had a place where he and Fan could camp.

"Sure. Building number ten to your left. Take any one of those open stalls. You can give your horse a bath if you want." His eyes flicked over Fan. Covered with dirt and sweat, she looked bedraggled compared to the resident horses. She had lost significant weight; it showed in her girth and withers. Her breast no longer had that layer of fat and muscle that made him tease her about how much she ate. And Jerry could no longer ignore the fact that some of her spirit had disappeared. It gave him a sick feeling, an ache in his chest to see how exhausted and dispirited she looked.

Jerry found the bathing area and washed her off, then brushed and combed her. He talked while he groomed her in the hope that his voice would perk her up. It had always rallied her before; now it seemed to make no difference. Fan ate some hay and rolled oats, but her demeanor and appearance screamed of an underlying fatigue that food and loving words could not touch. Once she finished eating, she lowered herself onto the fresh straw, heaved a big sigh, and put her head down. Sometimes she seemed more like a dog than a horse. Like Toby, the shepherd back at the Bar R, her sigh told Jerry that she considered her job done for the day.

The largest scab remained intact but it had begun to loosen around the edges. Riding her from Banning hadn't disturbed it, yet Jerry regretted having to ride Fan at all. As he watched her sleep, a part of him wished he'd taken Kevin up on his offer. Still, when he pictured getting out of Kevin's pickup at Pete's ranch and unloading her from the trailer, Jerry knew in his gut he could not cheat.

Fan and Jerry experienced a weariness that could not be remedied with a hearty meal, a cool bath, or a good night's sleep. Enduring heat that never let up and day-in and day-out traveling as many miles as their bodies could withstand had caused them to dig deep into their reserves. Both had called on muscle and nerve that had no more to give, yet give more they would have to do.

The Colorado River represented more than the border between two states. It symbolized the line that separated men from boys and tough horses from pretty horses. And the Mojave Desert embodied the place where a man was forced to face his deepest fears – the difference between conquest and surrender decided somewhere deep in his soul.

Jerry gazed down at his sleeping horse. "We're almost there, girl, hang on for a little while longer."

# 32

## Rose Bowl Grass Tastes Better

*Los Angeles Times*, June 20, 1946 // Head of Paramount's $1.1M Salary Highest in Nation // Soviet Move to Yugoslav Border Puts U.S. Army on Alert // Friends of Generals and Colonels By-Pass War Assets Administration Freeze, Purchase Surplus Planes

When Jerry awoke, Fan was standing up munching on hay she hadn't finished the night before. "You're up, and you look a little better." She did look better. He did, too. He'd used the shower, shaved, and put on his faded set of clean clothes. His hair had grown down to his collar again. He combed it back and quickly put his Stetson on to keep it in place.

Jerry and Fan rode under the arch onto Foothill Boulevard just as the sun came up. They headed due west along the front of orange grove properties. Orchards lined both sides of the wide boulevard, interrupted occasionally by houses with fenced pastures in front. They encountered fewer and fewer groves the farther west they rode. Business and apartment complexes replaced orchards, which forced them to ride on the edge of the boulevard and dodge cars racing by. By midafternoon Jerry felt spent. Fan's slow pace told him she felt the same. "It's too early in the day to be tired," Jerry reminded himself.

Fatigue never fully replenished added its weariness to the previous day and the day before that, combining with all the days of the journey like rainwater collecting in a barrel. Increasing in insidious increments, Jerry's and Fan's tiredness threatened to overwhelm the vessel. Early evening found them thirty miles west of San Bernardino in the tiny town of San Dimas. The minute he spotted Buddy's Burgers, Jerry gratefully patted Fan's neck and told her to stop. Neon flashed "Hamburgers, Fries, Fresh-Squeezed Orange Juice." He hadn't had a hamburger since leaving Oklahoma; just looking at the sign made his mouth water. He sat at a picnic table outside with Fan's reins wrapped around the bench leg. The mammoth twenty-five-cent hamburger tasted delicious, the ten-cent order of fries were crisp and hot, and the orange juice was ice cold. Jerry inhaled the food and had a refill of juice. A sign in the window advertised for a new employee. "Help Wanted, $.75/hr." Jerry eyed it as he downed the last of his drink. *I'd give anything to work here for about a week and have all the hamburgers, fries, and orange juice I could hold.*

Fan caused a stir being tethered so close to the sidewalk. Cars slowed and people gawked out their windows; kids on bicycles stopped. A little girl eating an apple walked by with her mother. She stopped near Fan and asked if she could give her apple "to the pretty horse." "Apples are Fan's favorite treat and I know for a fact she likes your calling her pretty." Jerry stood close and showed her how to protect her fingers while she fed Fan. Fan finished off the apple and delighted the little girl by nuzzling her for more. That night Jerry found a campsite a block north of the boulevard in San Dimas Canyon Park.

The next morning they got underway at sunup, just about the time Foothill Boulevard started coming to life. One small town flowed into the next with no break in between. Cars whizzed by on the two wide lanes of asphalt; buses lumbered by in both directions, spewing foul fumes. Though scant at first, the traffic seemed to double with each passing hour. By ten o'clock, Route 66 throbbed with life. Jerry had read that new cars were impossible to obtain and older cars were at a premium. Not in southern California. Thousands of them raced back and forth: new ones, old ones, fancy ones with whitewall tires, coupes, and huge sedans. Jerry saw more cars with their tops down in the first three hours of June 21st than he'd seen in his entire life. Hair flying, laughing and talking,

196

people raced by in convertibles with radios blaring. Jerry heard snatches of songs he recognized. People honked and waved and shouted hello. He sat tall in the saddle and felt a little like an alien.

Sunny and mild, the weather felt nothing like the overwhelming heat of the desert. Flowers of every kind were blooming in profusion; there were giant shade trees and lush green lawns and manicured grounds – so different from the desert plants and parched landscape Jerry had grown accustomed to seeing. In Monrovia, Foothill Boulevard dissolved into a fusion of orange groves, new developments, old Spanish-styled mansions, and businesses. Every block had an office or public building with pink bougainvillea winding its way up a wall onto the red-tile roof, leaving a trail of browned-tinged petals in its climb.

Two or three miles west of Monrovia, Jerry and Fan crossed into the bustling city of Pasadena and rode along Colorado Boulevard. Nestled at the base of the San Gabriel Mountains, Pasadena retained the strong Spanish and Mexican influence of its early heritage. Most of the buildings had thick walls, red-tile roofs, and arched porticos that faced the street. Unlike the busy street they rode along, the neighborhoods adjacent to Colorado Boulevard looked stately and serene. Jerry glanced down one broad street after another, amazed and impressed at the size of the rambling, Spanish-style mansions. They were two and three stories, each built in a different design but with similar materials – the effect pleasing to the eye.

Majestic sycamores and elms lined the streets, living symbols of the city's early beginnings. Gnarled limbs and broad green leaves embraced over the center of the streets and blocked out the sun. Jerry loved shade now. He had a whole new appreciation for it. His eyes sought out shade; he felt drawn toward it. Fan loved it, too. Though the temperature was mild, Jerry had a tug of war going with Fan, she trying to head for the shade of a front yard and he attempting to rein her back onto noisy Colorado Boulevard.

Day forty-nine of his journey. Jerry had spent the majority of the last forty-eight days in wide open spaces with only the sky, the earth, and his horse for company. Here he saw no open space except for the few remnants of orange orchards, most with "For Sale" signs on them. Every inch of ground had been consumed: covered with houses, businesses, and public buildings, dissected by fences, and lawned, graveled, asphalted, or surfaced with concrete. Even the mountains to the north had signs of development creeping up their slopes. Except for the distant mountaintops, Jerry could find no place for the eye to rest.

A city on the move, Pasadena. It was much larger to start with than Palm Springs, but, like the desert city, in the middle of growth it could not contain. Again Jerry saw no evidence of the supposed shortage of building materials. Everywhere he looked he saw new construction: schools, housing tracts, highways, churches, and a huge shopping center with yet another sign, "Future Home of Bullock's Department Store." Surrounded by cars, traffic, confusion and noise, people on bicycles and motorcycles – a motorized frenzy – Jerry felt overwhelmed by the pace. More than just agriculture disappearing, people scurrying about, or signs heralding the opening of a new school or department store, Pasadena projected a feeling, a sense that it would at any moment explode out of its boundaries – a gangly adolescent bursting out of his clothes before your very eyes. The pace wasn't the only harbinger of a new era. The people were as well: the way they looked, the way they dressed. Men and women in shorts, men in short-sleeved shirts, both rare in Oklahoma. Some men wore no shirts at all. Tanned and energetic women with their short hair styled in finger-waves and men with their hair Brylcreamed to perfection walked past Jerry and Fan with quick smiles and curious looks. He caught bits of their conversations: "Just got here from Iowa"; "enrolling in Cal Tech this fall on the GI Bill"; "got a job at the Jet Propulsion Lab"; "just moved into my new house"; "now that the war's over, I'm going to . . ."

The journey had lulled Jerry into an acceptance of solitude, of days on end with only Fan and a crackling campfire or the prairie and a starlit sky for company. And now he found himself smack in the middle of a world that was the antithesis of solitude, exactly like Jimmy Wakely said. Exciting and mind-boggling at the same time, it wowed Jerry as much as the Mojave Desert's blinding sun. Compared to the Bar R, southern California seemed like being on a different planet.

A sign announcing "Brookside Park, Turn Right One Mile" couldn't have come at a better time. Fan needed a place to rest, to get out of the traffic and have some water and food. Jerry turned onto Rosemont Avenue for a mile and then west into the park. Fan headed for the first shade she saw, but Jerry noticed something a lot more impressive than shade. A stadium loomed up out of the trees right in front of him. "Wow . . ." was all he could say as he gawked up at the edifice. "The Rose Bowl."

The structure dwarfed the trees and surroundings. Massive round cement columns spaced evenly around the perimeter supported the oblong-shaped stadium. Jerry dismounted and led Fan around the periphery, occasionally pausing to look up. Each time he stopped, Fan started to graze. "Sorry, girl. We'll stop just as soon as we walk all the way around." At the south end they encountered the main gate, signified by a large neon rose and the words "Rose Bowl" underneath. It was Friday noon and not a soul could be seen, but the gates were wide open. Jerry couldn't believe his eyes; he walked tentatively through the opening with Fan beside him. "Would you look at that, Fan," he whispered. "This is the most famous stadium in the country."

They entered a tunnel twenty or twenty-five feet long. At

the far end above the roof of the underground passage, Jerry could see rows of seats divided into sections, each section fifty rows tall at least. "I'll bet this place holds fifty thousand people." He considered stumbling onto the Rose Bowl a serendipitous accident, one of those things that happens once in a lifetime, and Jerry vowed not to miss it. The minute he climbed back on Fan she started moving forward. "You must want to see this place, too."

Fan walked through the tunnel's deep shade, and Jerry craned his neck at the ceiling, the walls, and the dirt floor. When they emerged into the dazzling sun, they stood at the top of a wide concrete ramp that sloped down seventy feet to a dirt track that encircled the stadium. "We just came through the players' tunnel, Fan." When Jerry's eyes adjusted to the bright light, he had a full view of the stadium.

From his vantage point high above the field, the goal posts and the hundred-plus yards of grass appeared to be small-scale versions of the real thing. Two horses, each harnessed to a cart, stood at the far left end of the track. Jerry shaded his eyes and squinted to make sure. "Trotters." A man knelt down next to one as he worked on the cart's wheel. Jerry and Fan rode down the ramp and onto the track, then Fan immediately strained left toward the horses. Jerry wanted to ride the long way around and take it all in, so he reined her to the right.

Once they were down on the track, his perspective totally changed. Everything seemed gigantic; the rows of seats looked like they stretched clear to the clouds. Jerry counted seventy rows in a section and more than twenty-five sections. From here the stadium looked more like it held a hundred thousand people. And the playing field, with every line painted white, straight, and perfect on the dark green grass, looked big enough to hold a battleship. Jerry had been to plenty of Guthrie High School football games and played on the school's field with his friends many times. He knew first-hand the length and width of an ordinary playing field. This

200

field was anything but ordinary. This was the Rose Bowl and as grand as anything he'd ever seen.

Jerry reined Fan up midway around and listened. *Quiet. So very quiet.* Down on the track, away from the noise and traffic outside, the stadium was a world unto itself, like the Palo Duro to the plains above it. "What must it be like to play football here, to win a game in front of a hundred thousand cheering people?" he said softly. Jerry closed his eyes.

Perhaps it was the result of being tired to the point of exhaustion. Maybe it was knowing he and Fan had both cheated death not once, but so many times. It could have been the accumulation of experiences hitting him all at once. Or a little bit of all three; Jerry wasn't sure. But he heard it as surely as he felt the sun on his face. Cheering, faint at first, started like a rumble, then grew louder, coming from every direction. Then Jerry heard it full blown, just like he'd heard it over the radio on New Year's Day. Only these cheers weren't coming from a radio, and they weren't for football players from Alabama or USC. A thrill went down his spine. Above the crowd noise an announcer's booming voice reverberated throughout the stadium. *"Ladies and gentlemen of the Rose Bowl. Let's hear it for Jerry Van Meter and his horse, Fan, from Guthrieee, Oklahomahhh."*

With his eyes closed, Jerry drank it in – a hundred thousand people screaming and yelling, raining down applause on an ordinary cowboy and his extraordinary horse. Every nerve tingled, a sensation of triumph detonated his weariness and exploded it into thousands of tiny fragments. He sat ramrod straight in the saddle, heart hammering, arms raised in a sign of victory. Jerry caught his breath and held it – trying to forever stamp this moment in his memory. *We won. Dammitall, we won.*

Fan moved beneath him; Jerry exhaled and opened his eyes. Poof, the crowd and the cheers were gone. All was silent once more. The feeling stayed with him for a moment as he

201

glanced around the empty stadium, then it scattered into the warm California air like leaves caught in a breeze.

No longer able to ignore something good to eat, Fan headed for the lush grass on the field a few feet away. Jerry let her graze at the edge. "If ever a horse deserved to eat someplace special, it's you." He only let her eat a small amount because she pulled out the roots and all. Jerry dismounted and scuffed over the spot with his boot. He led Fan back onto the track and walked in the direction of the trotters. "All I want to know is, does Rose Bowl grass taste better?"

Still bent down and working on the cart, the man hadn't realized Jerry and Fan were on the floor of the stadium. When he heard them approach he stood up and turned around with a surprised look on his face. "Who in the world are you?"

"Just a tired Oklahoma cowboy on his way to Hollywood."

The man's surprised look gave way to a smile. "Do you know where you are?"

"Yup, the Rose Bowl, granddaddy of them all."

He laughed and offered his hand, introducing himself as the Rose Bowl caretaker. When Jerry told him about their journey, the caretaker invited them to rest a bit. "Do you think your horse could use some water and hay?"

"Fan can *always* use water and hay. Thanks."

The caretaker broke open a bale and piled some hay on the edge of the grass. "You look pretty worn out, might as well rest while your horse has something to eat. This trip sounds interesting. I'd like to hear more about it."

Jerry removed Fan's saddle and she rolled like a puppy on the lush grass. He and the caretaker chuckled watching her; Fan rubbed her head back and forth in the grass. "Now I can tell everybody, without lying, that both of us made it into the end zone of the Rose Bowl."

Fan got up and drank her fill then moved to the pile of hay. The sun felt warm, and the grass as thick and soft as a bed. Jerry stretched out on his side, his head propped on his hand.

He asked all kinds of questions about the Rose Bowl, the stadium, about the games that had been played and the famous players who had played there. The caretaker knew it all. He was hired during the stadium's construction and had been there for its first game in 1923. Now, twenty-three years later, he was in charge of Rose Bowl maintenance.

The stadium seated 83,677 people, the approximate population of the city of Pasadena. It might be enlarged again in the next couple of years, he said, to one hundred thousand seats. USC won the first game played in the stadium in 1923 over Penn State, fourteen to three. The caretaker's favorite game took place in 1942 when Oregon State hung on in a close game over Duke: twenty to sixteen. "I like high-scoring games, but for some reason we don't get those in this bowl. That game didn't have a lot of points scored, but you didn't know up to the last minute whether Oregon State or Duke would pull it off. That made it exciting. Did you hear the game this year?"

"I did. Surprised me that USC got beat," Jerry said.

"Me, too. USC has played here more than any other school, nine times in the last twenty-three years and undefeated up to that game. Those Alabama boys felt pretty proud of themselves."

The soft grass and warm sun made it difficult for Jerry to get up and leave. Fan had finished off her hay and fallen asleep. Jerry would have liked to take a nap, too, but Hollywood waited. The end of the journey was at hand.

# 33

## End of the Journey

*Daily Variety*, June 21, 1946 // Jerry Lewis Discovers Singer Dean Martin in Atlantic City // Elizabeth Taylor Shares Top Billing with Canine in *The Courage of Lassie* // Newcomer Kirk Douglas, A Rising Star

With the traffic very heavy, Jerry and Fan made slow progress after leaving the Rose Bowl. It was Friday afternoon and it seemed that everyone in Los Angeles had someplace to drive. At the western edge of Pasadena, Route 66 turned southwest, aiming towards its final destination in Santa Monica. Leaving the famous highway, Jerry and Fan continued due west toward the southern edge of North Hollywood. They traveled on whatever street had the least amount of traffic, sometimes ending up in neighborhoods with children playing baseball. It made for slow going.

Jerry had Kevin Lamb's note with Pete's address on it. The verbal directions he'd given had been vague. "Try to find Camarillo Street. Keep going until you get to a corner with this hacienda-looking house with a pasture and a big barn. Turn right just past the barn. You can't miss it. Pete's place isn't too far, maybe five miles from there."

Jerry tried to remember Kevin's instructions after the initial turn he'd said to take. They had been standing by Kevin's trailer when he talked about Pete's place. Jerry grudgingly admitted he remembered more about what Kevin said about date palms than directions. Their conversation had taken place four hours after Jerry and Fan walked in off the desert; most of that conversation had been lost to fatigue.

Jerry found Camarillo Street around six P.M. and the hacienda house with the barn a few minutes later. He turned right

and quickly discovered the reason for Kevin's vague directions: a farming neighborhood in the process of being gobbled
up by the city. The area was a labyrinth of city lots, houses
with adjoining pastures, and dead-ends. Not all roads had
signs. On some of the streets that did have signs, the names
changed at an intersection or at a bend in the road.

Admitting he didn't remember any of what Kevin had told
him, Jerry searched using what he considered a systematic
pattern. When that plan did not produce results, he stopped
and asked for assistance. The first gentleman he asked didn't
recognize the address or Pete Wilson's name. Another helpful
resident looked up Pete's name in his telephone book but
found no listing.

Jerry retraced his way through several streets. They had
twenty minutes of sun left and maybe an hour of daylight after that. Jerry was exhausted, and Fan was, too. He considered making camp in one of the pastures and starting his
search the following morning, but tomorrow was Saturday,
June 22, the fiftieth day. He had promised himself that he
would beat that deadline if he could. He intended to keep that
promise.

The last resident Jerry asked mentioned an area where he
thought the ranch might be. "About two or three miles that
way," he said, pointing northeast. "I kinda remember horse
trailers going by here in that direction, but I've never been up
there."

Jerry rode to the northernmost street he had already
searched and turned east, then rode for another mile. He tried
two or three more streets. Still nothing. Directing Fan around
a corner and east along a gravel road bordered on one side by
an orchard and a pasture on the other, Jerry saw Pete's house
– just as Kevin had described it. A mailbox at the edge of the
road with the name "P. Wilson" on it confirmed their find.

What a welcome sight! The house sat amidst the best that
southern California had to offer, just what Jerry had promised

Fan when he wasn't at all sure they would find their way out of the desert. Surrounded by lush pasture with a creek ambling its way across the property, Pete's ranch had trees of every shape and size casting magic shade over untrimmed grass. Fruit trees, towering sycamores, elms with huge trunks, and tall airy trees with delicate leaves and purple flowers – more trees than Jerry had imagined at the height of his sun-baked fantasy. An arbor attached to the side of the house had grapevines intertwined through the latticework, with bunches of still-green grapes peeking through the spaces.

The house looked old, like the ranch house at the Bar R, only this one had two stories and was considerably bigger. Steep-roofed with fancy gables, it had white siding with weathered gray shutters and was obviously built by someone who appreciated space and design. The sun's last rays bathed it in color; the sunset glinting off the windows.

Jerry sat atop Fan at the edge of the quiet road and stared, trying to stamp the sight and this moment in his memory. The house, the shade trees, and the pasture symbolized their goal, the purpose and objective that had kept them going for the last forty-nine days. Hollywood, the magic place he had only heard about, fifteen hundred miles and a world away from the one he knew. Images of the last forty-nine days raced through his head in a silent movie rendering of the journey, speeding to this instant, this road, this house, and the realization that the adventure was over.

Jerry dismounted and stood holding Fan's reins, her head near his own. "I want you to remember this, girl. You did it. You're the one who got us here," he whispered.

Excitement, danger, exhaustion, laughter, loneliness, wonder – it was over now. Triumph, accomplishment, pride, fear, expectation – it could drive them no more. A release of breath held until the journey ended, and now it had, a sharp bittersweet moment.

Jerry led Fan over the grass toward the house. A spacious porch ran across the front. The door stood ajar and the wooden-framed screen that covered the opening needed a touch of paint. When Jerry spotted chairs on the porch – comfortable old wooden ones with cane bottoms and scuffed legs – he knew he was going to like this fellow Pete Wilson. Jerry knocked.

"Hold on a minute," came a booming voice from somewhere inside. A lanky silhouette appeared in the shadows and approached the screen. Jerry stepped back off the porch and stood near Fan. Pete Wilson came out of the house, his expression changing from curiosity to alarm. "What in the world, cowboy? You look like you – "

"We just rode in from Oklahoma." Jerry handed him the note from Kevin.

Pete led the exhausted pair to the barn and helped Jerry take care of Fan. Pete was an expert horseman, Jerry quickly decided, from the way he checked her over and from the supply of medicines and ointments he kept in the barn. With eyes closed, Pete ran his hands over her withers and chest and felt down her legs. "Lost a pretty good amount of weight, haven't you, girl."

He talked and worked like a vet; Pete had done this thousands of times. While they tended her, Jerry told him about meeting Kevin in Indio and briefly about their journey. When Pete replied, "Well, I'll be damned," exactly like Kevin had, Jerry had his first good laugh.

Pete Wilson, at just under six feet tall, was an imposing man. It showed in his carriage and his obvious strength. Lean, spare, and broad shouldered, he had gun-metal gray hair tinged with silver around his weathered face. Whether he was widowed, divorced, or never married, he didn't mention, saying only that he lived alone. He called this twenty acres home, the place where he trained and housed his best trick horses. But he had another, larger ranch, he told Jerry, in Frazier Park in the hills north of Los Angeles.

After Pete reassured Jerry that Fan was mainly suffering from exhaustion and dehydration and that she would improve with time and care, Jerry allowed himself to relax. Fan got what Jerry had promised her: a nice clean stall near other horses and plenty of cool water, hay, and rolled oats. "She'll be okay. What she needs now more than anything is rest," Pete said, patting her neck. As Pete led the way to the house, Jerry asked if he could use the phone.

Pete showed him the phone in the living room. He took a swing through the kitchen and pointed to the icebox. "Help yourself after you make your calls. This is your home as long as you'd like to stay. I want to hear your whole story from the beginning over coffee whenever you feel like waking up in the morning." He showed Jerry to an upstairs bedroom then pointed out the bathroom down the hall and handed him some towels. "I expect you to make a dent in that food in the icebox. Make yourself at home and I'll see you whenever you're good and rested. We wrapped up a film today and I don't have to work tomorrow, so we can do whatever you'd like. Maybe you'd like to see a little of Hollywood."

"I really appreciate your taking us in, it sure is ni – "

"It gets lonesome around here. I'm happy to have the company, and a real Oklahoma cowboy at that." Pete said goodnight and disappeared into his room at the other end of the hall.

Jerry called his parents in Guthrie first. With a two-hour time difference it was ten-thirty in Oklahoma, nearing his parents' bedtime. They would be in the living room reading and listening to music on the radio, and his brothers were most likely already asleep in the bunkhouse. The phone rang three times before he heard his mother's voice. Jerry's heart quickened as the operator asked her if she would accept the charges for a long distance call from a Jerry Van Meter in Hollywood, California.

"Most certainly," came her firm reply. He heard her calling his father. "Vearl, come quick, it's Jerry."

He spilled out his news in one breath. "I made it, Mom. I'm here in Hollywood. We did it in forty-nine days. We won."

"Jerry, I am thrilled! And so very proud of you, son. Are you okay? You sound exhausted." Jerry assured her he felt fine, tired but fine. "My, my, it's hard to imagine you being in Hollywood, California. That is so far away."

Jerry asked about his brothers, and then his father got on the phone. Vearl sounded relieved and genuinely happy to hear from him. He asked Jerry if the desert had been tough. Jerry promised to tell him all about it if he would make him a big bowl of fresh peach ice cream when he returned. That brought loud laughter – an unusual response for his father. "I'll take you up on that. Congratulations, son. What you did is a big accomplishment. You should be very proud."

The respect in his father's voice and the compliment made Jerry take a deep breath. He closed his eyes, allowing a new vision of himself to emerge as he listened. Their short conversation melted away a lifetime of father-son tension between two very different individuals.

Jerry made his second call to Frank Eaton's place in Perkins, Oklahoma. His mother said Rolla and Frank were visiting there for a few days. Frank's daughter, Orpha, answered the phone. She accepted the charges and then called her father. It took a few minutes for him to understand that it was Jerry on the phone, calling from Hollywood.

Frank sounded half-asleep. "Jerry, is that you?"

"It's me, Frank. Sounds like I woke you up."

"I might a been noddin' off in my chair. Did I hear right? Did Orpha say you was callin' from Hollywood?"

"Dammitall, I sure am. We made it, Frank."

Jerry had to hold the phone away from his ear. Frank started whooping and hollering, then called to Rolla. "Rolla! Get your sorry hide over here. I got a *real* cowboy on the line." Frank bombarded Jerry with questions, not waiting to hear one answer before asking another. "Hold on a minute, Jerry.

Your grandpa is slower 'n molasses in January." Frank turned away from the phone. "Put a little pepper in your step, Rolla."

Jerry expected to hear his grandfather's voice. Instead he heard Rolla and Frank laughing and talking with Orpha. Finally Rolla came on the phone, shouting as always. "I knew right from the beginning you'd do it. I am proud of you, Jerry. I just wish Charlie Goodnight could be here. He'd be proud, too, son."

"You never told me how much you'd win if I won, but from the sounds of it it must be a lot." Jerry shook with silent laughter as the reactions came in. He began to realize what he and Fan had just accomplished and it felt good.

"I'm not hollering about the money. That ain't worth a tinker's damn. You proving what a real cowboy can do is what we're excited about. You done more than me 'n Frank ever did."

"What do you mean? I thought this was the same as you two riding up the Goodnight-Loving Trail except for a herd."

Rolla suddenly sounded serious. "We've been talkin' about that. With Jimmy going on like he did, I guess I got rattled. When I made the bet I didn't stop to think about us having a remuda, our horses gettin' to rest. We had a bunch of cowhands to back us up if we got in trouble. You and Fancy did it all by yourselves, one horse the whole . . . by the way, is she okay?"

"Fan is going to be fine, Grandpa."

Never in his twenty years had Jerry heard his grandfather as excited or happy, or as talkative. Rolla recited Jimmy Wakely's phone number at his ranch in the San Fernando Valley and insisted that Jerry call him immediately. "Make sure to have Jimmy call me as soon as you hang up. I got a little braggin' to do." Frank shouted good-bye from the background before Rolla hung up.

By the time he dialed Jimmy's number, the enormity of their trip had sunk in. A little girl identifying herself as Lindalee answered the phone. "Just a minute." Jerry heard her put the phone down, her young voice becoming distant. "Daddy, it's a fellow from Oklahoma, says his name is Jerry . . . something. He wants to talk to you."

Jerry recognized Jimmy's voice. "I'll just bet you do," he chuckled. "You calling me from someplace in Arizona to come and pick you up?"

Now Jerry laughed. "No. I'm happy to say I am practically in your backyard. Sorry to call so late but I just hung up from talking to Grandpa. He insisted I call you right now and let you know I made it. You're supposed to call him as soon as we finish. I'll warn you, you're in for some bragging." Jerry gave Jimmy the Perkins number.

"I've always admired Rolla, liked him even when he's cantankerous. Your granddad won the bet fair and square, so I'll just have to listen to him brag." Jimmy sounded genuinely pleased. "How about coming out to the ranch tomorrow? I want to hear all about your ride, and I'd like you to meet Inez and the kids."

"I'm staying here in Hollywood with Pete Wilson, the head stuntman for Republic Pictures. He said he just wrapped up a picture today. I'll see if maybe he could drive me out to your place tomorrow."

"Make it in the afternoon and plan on staying for supper. Inez will treat you to some good homecooking. I'd like to meet Pete Wilson. I've heard about him from Wayne Burson, my stunt double. Wayne says he's one of the best."

"I'll check with him in the morning and call to let you know. You can give us directions then."

"You do that. And Jerry?" Jimmy said.

"What?"

"I didn't think *anybody* could make that ride in fifty days, but Rolla said you could, Frank, too. Your grandfather never doubted you for a minute. He has every right to be proud, and so do you. You are a cowboy clean through just like he said.

And that Goodnight tradition? I'll tell Rolla not to worry. It's in fine shape."

Jerry hung up and sat in the darkened room, allowing Jimmy's words to register. How embarrassed he'd felt seeing him that evening after the parade. Trying to avoid any discussion of the navy or himself. That evening seemed a lifetime ago. Jerry didn't feel embarrassed anymore.

Following Pete's instructions, Jerry made himself a huge sandwich from fixings he found in the icebox. He had his first hot shower in forty-nine days, with real shampoo and good-smelling soap. By the time he crawled into bed, fatigue had taken over; he could no longer keep his eyes open.

When Jerry stretched out and weariness enveloped him, it did so on a comfortable mattress with clean sheets and a soft pillow. *This is indescribable.* Before he could surrender to sleep, he kept the last promise he'd made to himself. "Thank you, Lord, for making this trip with me and Fan. It turned out to be the hard way, but thanks to you, we made it alri . . ." Sleep captured the last of the cowboy's prayer.

The End

CALIFORNIA

Fresno

Mojave
Desert

Hollywood
Pasadena
San Bernardino
Los Angeles
Banning
Palm Springs
Indio
Desert
Center
Blythe

Pacific
Ocean

Colorado River

San Diego

0    50    100 mi.
0    80    160 km.

# Epilogue

Pete Wilson took Jerry in without a moment's hesitation, opening his heart and home to a fellow cowboy, one of his own kind. Within a few days after Jerry's arrival, Pete invited Jerry to accompany him to Republic Pictures Studios in Hollywood. They hired Jerry on the spot as a wrangler, riding horses and driving runaway stagecoaches and covered wagons in western B movies.

Following their visit with Jimmy Wakely at his San Fernando Valley ranch the day after his arrival, Jerry and Pete trailered Fan up to Pete's ranch in the hills north of Los Angeles. Pete asked the caretaker who looked after Pete's herd and a few other horses they boarded to take care of Fan. She spent a month running free on the sixty-acre ranch. When Jerry saw her again the change was remarkable. She had gained much of her weight back and, to his relief, she acted like her old feisty self. They took her back to Pete's ranch in North Hollywood to continue her recovery.

Jerry made sure he delivered on his promise to Fan in the desert. Fan enjoyed warm sun and a cool breeze; she had plenty of shade, all she could eat and drink, the companionship of other horses, and what she loved most – attention. While Jerry spent his days making movies, one of Pete's neighbors, a girl of fourteen on summer vacation, began visiting Fan. Her morning visits soon turned to lengthy daily visits, then her entire summer became devoted to Fan. The girl lavished attention on her, grooming Fan until she sparkled like a show horse, feeding her oats and her favorite treats, teaching her tricks, and finally riding her around the grounds of Pete's ranch.

Fan blossomed under the loving girl's care. The affection between them flourished until even Jerry could not ignore it. She was an accomplished rider and told Jerry her dream was to become a trick rider, riding in rodeos, western shows, and county fairs. She and her father had been looking for a steady horse for two years – one that would be responsive and loving, not skittish. She wanted a strong, unflappable horse like Fan. At summer's end, Fan's new friend told Jerry shyly that she had fallen in love with his beloved Osage Indian mare.

Jerry stayed with Pete at his North Hollywood home and worked for Republic Pictures until a strike in December 1946 brought film production at the studios to a halt. The time had come to go home. Jerry knew the return trip to Oklahoma by train would be difficult on Fan, and the life awaiting her would never hold what Jerry knew this special horse deserved.

The young girl offered Fan affection, the constant attention she craved, and the care befitting a royal breed – everything Jerry wanted for her but could not give. He sold Fan to the young girl in December 1946 shortly before leaving for Oklahoma. Another bittersweet moment.

Jerry loved Fan. "The best horse I've ever known," he said during our first interview. He never saw or heard of Fan again, yet more than fifty years later, the mention of her name brings a smile and a wistful look to his face. Together they shared a unique experience, riding fifteen hundred miles to win a bet, to prove a point, to honor tradition. An experience shared by cowboys of old? Possibly. An event duplicated in the postwar era? Not of which this author is aware.

Jimmy Wakely paid off the bet to Rolla Goodnight, the amount of which they took to their graves. Rolla and Frank, proud symbols of the era they personified, continued cowboying together almost to the end. Frank lived to be ninety-eight and died at home in Perkins on April 8, 1958. Rolla, devastated by the loss of his friend of seventy-five years, survived another fourteen months. He died in Guthrie on January 8, 1960, at age eighty-nine. Jimmy Wakely, who experienced a successful singing career after his movie career ended, died at age sixty-eight in Mission Hills, California, in 1982.

A widower now, Jerry is seventy-three years old. He lives in Kalispell, Montana, where he has a clear view of the Rocky Mountains from his living-room window. A retired miner, Jerry was, and always in his heart will be, a cowboy.

Jerry's adventure – The Great American Cowboy Rides Again – proved something to an astute movie star who was part of the coming tide and to two old cowboys belonging to the age it replaced. By his journey, Jerry showed that an ordinary man and an exceptional horse can lift themselves above the crowd and accomplish an extraordinary feat.

In 1946 the United States was stirring and thumping its chest in celebration after four years of waiting and holding its breath while the world's eyes and ears were on Europe and the Pacific. A pivotal decade in America, the forties came to a close witnessing the largest spurt in births in U.S. history – the baby boomers – and the promise of a dazzling future.

Hollywood, after the war, exploded with an influx of soldiers and sailors, truck drivers, cowboys, secretaries, and clerks, all swept up in a make-believe world. Nothing more than kids, they came from large cities and small towns, from mundane jobs that suddenly seemed stifling. Hollywood became a magnet for young, beautiful people determined to succeed. They banded together and energized a magic city that promised money, freedom, and fame. And the names and films of those *kids*, whose tenacity and talent persevered, are part of our culture.

America's sudden new role as world leader propelled the country and its citizens along in a fast-paced tide of exciting discoveries and social progress. In that context, Jerry's adventure was a step back in time to the nineteenth century, a personal quest that tested limits, nerve, and heart; his only rewards: words of praise, his memories, and his private feelings of accomplishment.

From a vantage point at the start of a new century, Jerry's journey speaks not just of courage, determination, and integrity, but of a national innocence lost, of new values and definitions. Still, after over fifty years of unparalleled progress, we continue to search for those unselfish men upon whom an indefinable light shines – men we like to call *heroes*.

The young cowboy from Oklahoma shared a brief moment in the make-believe world of Hollywood and then returned to the world he knew. Jerry Van Meter started his adventure a confident boy of barely twenty. The journey, its travails and triumphs, produced a courageous and humble man, and a story this author is proud to have told.